October 1, 2010
For Mark & Susan,
in loving
friendship.

Paul

Political Engagement as Biblical Mandate

Political Engagement as Biblical Mandate

PAUL D. HANSON

CASCADE *Books* • Eugene, Oregon

POLITICAL ENGAGEMENT AS BIBLICAL MANDATE

Cascade Books
An Imprint of Wipf and Stock Publishers
199 W. 8th Ave., Suite 3
Eugene, OR 97401

www.wipfandstock.com

ISBN 13: 978-1-55635-515-8

Cataloging-in-Publication data:

Hanson, Paul D.

Political engagement as biblical mandate / Paul D. Hanson.

ISBN 13: 978-1-55635-515-8

viii + 160 p. ; 23 cm. Includes bibliographical references and indexes.

1. Bible—Hermeneutics. 2. Christianity and politics—Biblical teaching. 3. Covenant theology—Biblical teaching. I. Title.

BS680 P45 H35 2010

Manufactured in the U.S.A.

Contents

Introduction

The infusion of public debate with religious arguments, though as genuinely American as apple pie, has in recent times generated a carefully articulated position for "checking religion at the door" before a citizen enters the public forum.[1] It would appear that at least in part this position is the liberal's response to the success that has accompanied the Religious Right's discovery of its public voice. As a result of the collective efforts of a broad coalition of Christian Evangelicals, elections have been influenced if not determined, judicial appointments have undergone uncharacteristically rigorous litmus tests, and local and state school boards have been pressured into aggressive tactics in the selection of science curricula and textbooks. The ironically un-liberal argument from the left seems to be this: Though for over two centuries, American political decisions have been hammered out on the anvil of religio-political debate, the civic manner in which that debate historically has been conducted is being threatened by a sanctimonious appeal to purportedly uncontestable biblical warrants for criminalizing abortion, banning gay marriage, and mandating the teaching of creationism in public schools. The argument goes on to claim that with the maturing of our culture into a post-Christian secularism and the increase in religious and ideological diversity (e.g., presently in the U.S. Muslims have come to outnumber Episcopalians), the free expression of religious ideas in public debate exacerbates civic tension and undermines a society's ability to solve its most urgent problems.

In the pages that follow I seek to make the case that religiously informed thought has played and can continue to play a constructive role in the public forum over domestic and international issues that are weighted with moral content. At the same time, the stark fact that religion has often been introduced into public controversies in

1. Richard Rorty, "Religion as Conversation-stopper."

a manner more manipulative and coercive than civil and engaging underlines the need to clarify what style of religious argument is proper, legal within our First Amendment tradition, and helpful in relation to the health and vitality of the Republic. Beyond the issue of what can be called the etiquette of public discourse is the equally controversial issue of the nature of a religious tradition's authority within the public realm, and it should be granted from the outset that in a religiously diverse society, all scriptures must be treated on an equal plain. As we shall see, widely divergent views emerge, ranging from the fundamentalist view that a given Scripture infallibly circumscribes divinely revealed truth that is normative for all human questions and social issues to the view that all scriptures are to be understood strictly as the products of human authors.

Inasmuch as my view occupies a position between the fundamentalist/absolutist and the humanist/relativist views, I shall seek to articulate a position that accepts a particular scriptural tradition, the Jewish-Christian tradition, as a reliable witness to divine purpose for human existence and the entire created order while affirming at the same time that any interpreter of that tradition participates fully in the epistemological limits that define the viewpoint of every human, no matter what his or her religion or philosophical position.

Because both facets of the problem facing the person of faith who seeks to explain the relevance of Scripture for our life together in a diverse society are complicated and resistant to any comprehensive answer, the chapters that follow are best viewed as explorations. But rather than haphazard, they seek to probe several of the questions that I believe lie at the heart of the question, what light does the Bible shed on life in our nation and world today? In terms of my personal scholarship, it can be viewed as a "trial balloon" sent out into the open skies of the public square in hope for constructive criticism and lively debate.

1 *In Search of a Biblically Based Political Theology*

OUR TASK

It has become common parlance to speak of a global economy. Whether in boom times or recessions, the interdependency of nations—large and small, industrial and developing—is evident. The banking crisis that struck the member-states of the G10 in 2008 threatened the financial stability not only of the world's richest countries, but had crippling effects on nations that even in more normal times were finding it impossible to service their debts and provide minimal care for their poor and infirm. In the area of economics, the world clearly is woven tightly into a single web. As much as individual states would like to step outside of this web, they are bound as economic partners "for better or for worse, for richer, for poorer, in sickness and in health."

In the meantime, many people of faith live in a world that is confined to their particular congregation, denomination, or locality. Charity is directed to the immediate neighbor and the spiritual family is coterminous with one's own parish, whereas references to Darfur, Somalia, and Pakistan register with the hollow sound of far away places. Such are the fruits of a spirituality that has become increasingly individualistic, of an ecclesiology excluding any concept of the individual congregation being part of a worldwide network, of salvation construed as a gift of eternal life given exclusively to those adopting a particular set of beliefs.

Fortunately, the classic biblical view of the church as a universal phenomenon has not been extinguished completely, but lives on in congregations in Minnesota vitally connected with sister congregations in Tanzania, among doctors devoting months of pro bona

1

service in disaster areas throughout the world, and within organizations raising millions of dollars for food, medicines and agricultural equipment in striving to serve "the least of these my brethren."

Perhaps the need to re-experience the world as one global family of God's children is especially urgent in a country like the United States where endemic isolationism fosters a hegemonous sense of superiority. To the extent that engaging in the commerce of religious and ethical ideas is entertained, it is construed as exporting aspects of the world's most advanced civilization to more benighted parts of the world.

Although such a parochial worldview can be challenged both by rigorous news reporting and commentary such as one gets on NPR and PBS and insightful fictional and nonfictional books like Khaled Hosseini's *The Kite Runner,* Greg Mortenson and David Relin's *Three Cups of Tea,* Elias Chacour and David Hazard's *Blood Brothers,* and Rory Stewart's *The Places in Between,* Mark Twain's antidote perhaps remains the most effective for the fortunate minority that can afford it, namely, the exposure of "innocents abroad" to other cultures through travel. Three times in the last several years, my own "innocent" eyes have been opened thanks to invitations to lecture in South Africa, the Philippines, and India. In each case, what modest scholarly contribution I could offer was repaid many times over by lessons taught by courageous women and men who in their struggles for justice and acts of compassion have demonstrated to the world the profound relevancy of the Bible for contemporary political policy and action.

One cannot avoid the question: "What is it about the culture of creaturely comforts and *assumed* security that turns our attention inward and leads to a dulling of the sense of shared global humanity and the preciousness of every single newborn baby?" The answer comes through pilgrimage to Nelson Mandela's cell on Bird Island, through conversation with a Jesuit priest fasting in solidarity with Manila's impoverished shanty dwellers, and in the testimony of a parish pastor in a district of India threatened by anti-Christian prejudice and violence. In the visitor's homeland, liberty is taken for granted and demands little in return; in the host society, liberty is a daily struggle demanding great courage and entailing suffering.

In the visitor's homeland, a sense of the contemporary meaning of Hebrew slaves escaping willy-nilly from a ruthless oppressor must be sought through a scholarly exercise; in the host society it is encountered daily in crowded streets and marketplaces. In the visitor's homeland, the thought of a God who would sacrifice his own son to win back rebellious children hell-bent on their own destruction is about as comprehensible as forfeiting all one's possessions and giving them to the poor; in the host society only *such* a God can offer hope to those experiencing all earthly forms of power as agents of their exploitation.

The reflections found in this book arose specifically and concretely from one visitor's encounter with his hosts. For the gracious and courageous Christians with whom I became friends, the reality of a global spiritual family is as real and essential to humanity's survival as a healthy global economy. Thus, for example, when Fr. Victor Salanga invited me to address the Annual Convention of the Philippine Catholic Biblical Society under the theme of "Scripture and the Quest for a New Society," he had in mind not a new society designed for his country alone, but a society defined by the universality of the Kingdom of God. And he was not timid in making the connection between the *two realms*: "Our Bible has much to say about economics and politics."

Much indeed, enough to fill many volumes, but the advantage of a short book is that it behooves one to move immediately to the heart of the matter. And as I see it, the heart of the matter pulsates with a central truth that flows through the length and breadth of Scripture: For the person of faith and for the faith community, there is but *one government* to which we owe our ultimate allegiance, and that is the universal government whose Ruler is the author and source of all that is just, compassionate, and respectful of the dignity of every creature. Our shared citizenship in that regime places upon us concrete responsibilities in relation to our specific nation-states. And the common task that thereby unites Christians throughout the world is unambiguous and urgent, namely, to clarify the mandate of Scripture for all those whose political starting point is the Bible, to aid one another in drawing forth implications for domestic and international crises that transcend nationalism and political ideology, and to forge strategic alliances with justice-loving adherents of other religions in obedience to the Creator and Redeemer of all families, creeds, and nations.

A HISTORY OF NATIONALISTIC IDOLATRY

If there is one fundamentally important lesson that nations have not learned from the tragic events of the past, it is the lesson of resisting the temptation of confusing human rule with divine rule. Let us consider the policy adopted by the United States towards the fledgling independence movement in the Philippines at the beginning of the twentieth century as an example.

In pre-colonial times, the inhabitants of the Philippine archipelago regarded the forests, fields, and waters as communal property, to be cultivated for the good of all. Of course there were differences in status between clan heads and their subjects, but one pictures a gentler way of life than the harsh conditions imposed by the importation of European feudalism by the Spanish, the ill-effects of which still afflict the lives of a large percentage of the Philippine populace. After the liberation struggles of the early 1890s were interrupted by the Cuban revolution and then the Spanish-American war, memory of their own nation's earlier struggle against colonialism was lost by President McKinley and his cabinet as they strove to enhance the competitive edge of the U.S. in the increasingly lucrative maritime trade routes connecting East and West. In the congressional debates of that time over the annexing of the Philippines, national hubris rose to new heights, as illustrated by the speech in defense of U.S. intervention by Senator Albert Beveridge:

> God has not been preparing the English-speaking and Teutonic peoples for a thousand years for nothing but vain and idle self-contemplation and self-admiration. No! He has made us the master organizers of the world to establish system where chaos reigns . . . He has made us adept in government that we may administer government among savage and senile peoples. Were it not for such a force as this the world would relapse into barbarism and night. And of all our race He has

marked the American people as His chosen nation to finally lead in the regeneration of the world.[1]

Such imperialistic policy arises out of the blasphemous identification of one nation's destiny with divine purpose. In ancient Egypt the corollary was found in the belief that the Pharaoh was the incarnate god Horus. Rome based its authority to impose the *Pax Romana* on the clans and nations it conquered on the claim of Augustus and his successors to be divine. The persistent tendency for the U.S. to claim the right to determine the political destiny of other nations rests on a typological connection, namely, that it is the new Israel. This was a notion the Puritans brought with them from England, but it matured in the nineteenth century in step with the growth of U.S. imperialism and was christened by John L. O'Sullivan in 1839 as "Manifest Destiny."[2]

The reason why the concept of "manifest destiny" must concern us here is this: The primary warrant enlisted in its defense is the Bible. At the apex of Spanish colonial power, conquest was understood not simply as the means of advancing the cause of Philip's kingdom, but as an instrument for the spread of the Kingdom of God to Central and South America and the Philippines. In recent U.S. history, the most ardent supporters of the *Pax Americana* in the Middle East and in East Asia have been the leaders of the Religious Right, that is, those religious and political figures who claim to understand the bearing of Scripture on international developments.

Citizens of nations that have not yet become as secularized as countries like France and Sweden but retain the biblical story as part of their own epic understanding of nationhood face a particular challenge: The Bible remains ensconced in the cultural ethos as a powerful warrant in political argumentation. And, as Willard Swartley has documented, it can be used with equal force on *opposite* sides of moral struggles involving issues such as war, slavery, and women's rights.[3] Any reflexive, uncritical invocation of biblical authority in defense of a policy or action that places millions of

1. Beveridge, speech delivered on January 9, 1900.
2. O'Sullivan, "The Great Nation of Futurity."
3. Swartley, *Slavery, Sabbath, War, and Women.*

people at risk must raise serious moral and theological concerns for all people of faith. Have not the testimonies of Dietrich Bonhoeffer and Desmond Tutu burned with sufficient clarity into our modern consciousness the urgent need to treat any political interpretation of the Bible with diligence and attentiveness to the critical scrutiny of interlocutors of all nations and creeds? Dare we lack the courage to name every self-serving domestication of the Bible an heinous act of nationalistic idolatry?

Harold Lindsell in 1976 published a book defending biblical inerrancy under the title, *The Battle for the Bible*.[4] Fifteen years later and from a very different, though no less deeply committed Christian perspective, James Davison Hunter authored a book bearing the title *Culture Wars: The Struggle to Define America*.[5] More recently, in a book titled *The Clash of Civilizations and the Remaking of World Order*, Harvard professor of government, Samuel Huntingdon, predicted increasing strife between the Muslim East and the Christian West leading to a decline of the latter and the emergence of China as a world power.[6] While these books differ widely with each other in their underlying assumptions and conclusions, they converge in painting a somber picture of a future in which religious and ideological differences will be a driving force in cultural and international conflict. Conscientious believers dare not stand by passively as imperious religious and political leaders exploit the Bible to defend reckless foreign policies in the pursuit of self-serving economic and geo-political objectives.

WHAT IS THE NATURE OF BIBLICAL AUTHORITY IN RELATION TO POLITICS?

What this question requires is a hermeneutic capable of translating the meaning of Scripture into contemporary political, social and economic relevance in a manner that is both in accord with the legal

4. Lindsell, *The Battle for the Bible*.

5. James Davison Hunter, *Culture Wars*.

6. Huntingdon, *The Clash of Civilizations and the Remaking of World Order*.

norms and social mores of a given society and faithful to the central tenets of the proponent's religious tradition. The problem facing the modern world resides not in a lack of efforts to apply various scriptures to world events, for we see ample examples within various branches of Islam, Christianity, and Judaism to inculcate and disseminate what is purported to be the political message of the deity. Rather, the problem is the nature of that application, or, to use the technical term again, the hermeneutic by which it is directed. Let us cite several examples to clarify the problem.

During his second term of office, Ronald Reagan, Commander-in-Chief of the world's mightiest nuclear power locked in the grips of a Cold War with the Soviet Union, shared his biblical "hermeneutic" with Israeli lobbyist Tom Dine: "You know, I turn back to your Old Testament and the signs foretelling Armageddon, and I find myself wondering if—if we're the generation that's going to see that come about. I don't know if you've noted any of these prophecies lately, but believe me, they certainly describe the times we're going through."[7] On the surface, these words remain cryptic, but read against the background of Hal Lindsey's bestseller, *The Late, Great Planet Earth*,[8] it seems that Reagan was envisioning the possibility of a coordinated attack by the Soviet Union and China on Israel, which would set in motion the end-time cataclysm of Armageddon, a scenario sure to provoke the U.S. to unleash its nuclear arsenal.

On January 14, 1991, President George H. W. Bush was on the eve of announcing whether the U.S. would attack Iraq in response to Saddam Hussein's invasion of Kuwait. His own Episcopal Bishop, Edmond Browning, had expressed his opposition to Desert Storm. That evening the President invited Evangelist Billy Graham to the White House. The next day CNN televised the pyrotechnical extravaganza of bombs falling on Baghdad. A year later the by then former President Bush had the opportunity to express his thanks at the annual meeting of The National Religious Broadcasters: "I want to thank you for helping America, as Christ ordained, to be 'a light

---

7. Quoted in *Jerusalem Post*, Oct. 28, 1983.

8. Lindsey, *The Late Great Planet Earth*.

unto the world.'"[9] What hermeneutic underlies this stingingly ironic scriptural reference? Is it simply an exploitation of biblical language in defense of a military action that was already etched in the sand? It is said that former presidential advisor Ralph Reed commented that he was glad that when he turned to the Christian faith his politics could remain unchanged. Is such a docile role of faith in relation to politics in accord with the examples of Christian leaders remembered by history for their acts of courage in times of crisis? What is the role of the Bible in relation to domestic and foreign policy? Is it simply to provide politically expedient justifications, or is it to provide a perspective free from ideological entanglements and open to chastening and reproof?

George W. Bush, in a Spring 2004 press conference, reflected on his Iraq war initiative with this theological statement: "Freedom is the Almighty's gift to every man and woman in this world. And as the greatest power on the face of the Earth, we have an obligation to help the spread of freedom."[10] On the face of it, this sounds like an admirable goal. But if it is a pious rationalization authorizing the U.S. to act unilaterally and without restraints in promoting a plan of geo-political control over the oil-rich countries of the Middle East, it raises the specter of national idolatry, the confusion of divine and national purpose. As the military occupation of Iraq became besmeared with the shocking photographs taken in the Abu Ghraib prison facility and the number of civilian and military causalities accelerated, the prophetic irony of George H. W. Bush's earlier remark in defense of stopping short of a full invasion of Baghdad in 1991 became shockingly apparent: "Trying to eliminate Saddam would have incurred incalculable human and political costs ... Had we gone the invasion route, the United States could conceivably still be an occupying power in a bitterly hostile land."[11]

Clearly, in the case of U.S. foreign policy, the Bible is not dismissed as an irrelevant relic of the past, for publicly vocal preach-

9. George H. W. Bush, Remarks at the Annual Convention of National Religious Broadcasters, January 27, 1992.

10. George W. Bush, press conference, April 13, 2004.

11. George H. W. Bush, in Bush and Scowcroft, *A World Transformed*, chap. 19.

ers claiming to be its true interpreters often are seated in places of honor among those who write and execute U.S. policy. But what sort of biblical message are they presenting, and what is the nature of the hermeneutic being applied by Presidents and their closest advisors. In the case of Reagan and the Bushes, the most charitable reading would be that they were simple, pure-hearted Christians applying biblical truth under the tutelage of preeminent religious leaders. A more cynical reading would ask whether they were being manipulated by Right Wing leaders like Jerry Falwell, Pat Robertson, and Karl Rove to advance, under the pretense of biblical faith, self-serving national policies that may be in tension with or even contradict central tenants of Scripture. While room for debate over such complex and controversial issues remains, what cannot be neglected is critical analysis of the hermeneutical and moral dimensions involved in the application of biblical warrants to political policy and the economic and military actions they promote.

Part of such analysis must be the examination of the dispensationalist theology that for over a century has shaped the global policy of some of Washington's most influential political leaders (including presidents, senators and representatives), and in the background their advisors (both official and informal) and influential and well-funded lobbyists. Though that task is too large for the present context, the initial observation can be made that the political theology that has been advanced by many influential religious and political leaders in the United States is theocratic, at times even resembling hermeneutical principles followed by Islamic fundamentalists and extreme religious Zionists like the followers of Meir Kahane and Baruch Goldstein. Held in common by these otherwise strange bedfellows is the assumption that Scripture—whether the Quran, the Tanak, or the Christian Bible—contains a political blueprint that they bear responsibility to promote in the realms of cultural mores and international policies. The exclusivist, theocratic nature of their program is illustrated by Tim LaHaye, co-author of the apocalyptic bestseller series, *Left Behind*: "No humanist is qualified to hold any governmental office in America—United States senator, congressman, cabinet member, State Department employee, or any other position that requires him think in the best interest of

America . . . [Christians] must vote in pro-moral leaders who will return our country to the biblical base upon which it is founded."[12] Paul Weyrich adds: "We're radicals working to overturn the present structure in this country—we're talking about Christianizing America."[13]

Thus far our illustrations of what can be characterized as the enlistment of Scripture for political purposes have been drawn from members of the Republican Party. When we turn our attention to Democratic leaders, we see another facet of the "culture war" that Hunter has studied. Quite generally, Democratic leaders have sought to avoid religious language. While he was at the apex of his campaign to become the presidential candidate of the Democratic Party, Howard Dean, who once explained that he withdrew from his church over a dispute about a bike path, offered the liberal rationale for avoiding religiously charged hot-button issues. The presidential race, he insisted, should stay away from the issues of "guns, God and gays" and focus on "jobs, healthcare, and foreign policy." To be sure, even before the sea change initiated by Barack Obama, we can find Democrats who did not hesitate to expose the spiritual and even biblical dimensions of their political thought. Notable was the candor with which Jimmy Carter revealed how his Christian faith influenced his decisions, and certainly his post-White House career as world spokesman for peace and advocate for the poor has demonstrated the staying power of his idealism. Bill Clinton began his presidency with biblical themes like covenant and community, themes that were translated into political action in the drive for healthcare reform (spearheaded aggressively by his wife Hilary, but failing to gain sufficiently wide support to be implemented), improvement of the nation's public school system, and tax relief for lower and middle-class Americans. Noteworthy as well was the zeal with which Clinton, as he approached the end of his second term in office, sought to bring the Israelis and Palestinians towards a lasting peace agreement at the Second Camp David. Unfortunately, a promising moment of hope vanished amidst the impeachment

12. LaHaye, *Mind Siege*, 86.

13. Paul Weyrich, Director of The Committee for the Survival of a Free Congress; quoted in Richley, *Religion in American Public Life*, 331.

proceeding stemming from the Monica Lewinsky affair, an episode exposing another dimension of the Bible/Politics dialectic, the dimension of private morality.

When one ponders that dimension and specifically the impact of moral turpitude on political process, the biblical paradigm that most readily comes to mind is the story of David and Bathsheba, even as the words that epitomize the potentially tragic impact of infractions in the realm of personal ethics on the realm of public duty were the words of divine judgment pronounced against David by the prophet Nathan: "Now therefore the sword shall never depart from your house" (2 Samuel 12:10). As in the case of biblical paradigms arising from episodes in public realms such as the judicial system, business practices, and international policy, however, the David/Bathsheba story does not provide a proof-text that can be applied mechanically to any contemporary event. The contribution it makes is more subtle, for one must remember that the biblical narrative goes on to describe how God continued to use David for his purposes. On the other hand, the warning against mechanical proof-texting is not an invitation to use the ambiguities that are a part of the fabric of biblical narrative to dismiss the personal realm as of no political significance. In the personal as in the wider public domain, human actions carry consequences. And it is for that reason that the community of faith studies the Bible using all of the methods at its disposal as well as the collective wisdom of the ages as it searches for the balance between judgment and pastoral concern for its leaders in their moments of moral failure.

To summarize our discussion of the issue of biblical authority in relation to politics, we can draw the following thoughts from recent U.S. history: Those who have been most explicit in enlisting the Bible in public discourse have tended to incorporate a hermeneutic that is absolutist and theocratic in nature, with the Bible functioning as a source of warrants for positions against abortion and gay marriage and in defense of assertive American foreign policy and a traditional definition of sexuality. The more muted hermeneutic characteristic of much, though not all, of the Democratic Party revolves around a strict application of the First Amendment to minimize the use of religious language in political debate.

The question arising out of this dichotomy is a challenging one: Is there a more adequate hermeneutic, one that will be faithful to the biblical heritage while yet remaining sensitive to the legal and cultural norms of a society characterized by religious and philosophical diversity? Before turning to this question, we need to examine the realm of politics in the Bible to discern the manner in which faith was applied to social and economic issues by our spiritual ancestors.

POLITICS IN THE BIBLE

While every endeavor to direct modern questions to ancient writings runs the risk of producing anachronisms, the basic fact remains that ancient Israel and the early Christian communities struggled with political, economic, and social issues not dissimilar to ones faced today, in relation to which they sought to find answers under the guidance of their scriptural traditions. What is less obvious, or ignored, by many students of the Bible is this: In contrast to the dominant cultures around them, the ancient Israelites did not view the divine realm as the source of a timeless design of government that was transmitted in the form of a state myth to temple officials. Indeed, the founding events of the Israelite community revolved around the repudiation of the myth of the Pharaoh inspired by encounter with a God embracing the cause of peasants and slaves. As a running account of Israel's relationship with the God who accompanied them and—when they allowed—directed them through the changing conditions of their historical existence, Israel's sacred writings took the form of an epic, elaborated with laws, psalms, laments, and proverbs. This dynamic, historical perspective of the people of Israel accounts for there being not one timeless political model in the Bible, but six, arising each in turn as Israel sought to tease out the political implications of God's rule for her national existence.

The first political model to emerge in Israel was theocratic in nature. It arose out of the question: How do we organize our life so as to reflect our origin in the act of a God who freed slaves and gave them a land and a future? In response to the continued efforts of Canaanite kings like Sisera to re-impose absolute monarchy upon them, they organized as a loose confederation of tribes and insisted that their only king was Yahweh. They expressed their cultic and political unity only in annual pilgrimages and in defensive battles, and even there the rallying point was Yahweh's reign over them. They devised laws and economic structures that expressed the equality of all citizens under the one divine Ruler, laws forbidding usury and its tendency to lead to debt slavery, the levirate marriage custom that secured for the widow economic security, and a structure of land tenure that divided use of the land equally among extended families and acted as a counter force to the accumulation of property by the wealthy at the expense of the poor by insisting that there was only one legitimate title holder, the very God who allotted the land equally to the clans in the first place!

The theocratic phase of Israel's history was remarkable in many ways. It introduced a new worldview in which the deity was viewed not as an absolute authority securing humans in a timeless social pyramid enforced by an earthly surrogate, the divine king or pharaoh, but as a guide present with humans in their earthly experiences. The nature of their God as liberator of slaves intensified the profound moral insight tracing back to Hammurabi and beyond, namely, the Chief Justice of the universe was the guardian and protector of the rights of the weak and vulnerable. This in turn set the standard upon which human governments were to be measured. The heart of God's people was to be fashioned out of justice and compassion that extended memory of the past to her daily life in the present. Though its idealistic notion of there being only one even-handed Ruler, Yahweh, shattered in practice on the ledges of a turbulent world, it lived on in principles that would be upheld as the basis for judging all of the forms of government to follow, principles of evenhanded justice, equal distribution of wealth, and care for the poor and infirm. Of specific interest are two concepts, for though they were compromised in the course of subsequent biblical history almost beyond recognition by resurgent elitism and corruption, they continue to convict unjust governments to this day.

One is the concept of נחל ה (*nahalah*), the division of the use of the land equally among the clans and the insistence that because God alone held title, those who accumulated land through exploitation of the common farmer were guilty of a crime against heaven! Given similarly communal notions of land usage in pre-colonial tribes and clans in the Americas, in Africa, and in Southeast Asia, it is wise to ponder what potential contributions a particular culture's pre-modern history might contain for future reforms. It is interesting to observe, for example, the inspiration that the custom of open discourse in the pre-Christian tribal counsels of South Africa imparted to Nelson Mandela's revolutionary concept of Truth and Reconciliation. When we come to the fourth biblical political model, the sapiential, we shall see how a biblically based politics can be open to such contributions from spheres beyond the traditional belief system.

The other concept worth noting from the period of ancient Israel's theocracy is the Jubilee. Besides the forgiveness of debt and the release of slaves in the seventh year, in the fiftieth year observance of the Jubilee stipulated return of lost properties to their rightful owners as an essential part of the land's being restored to its original divinely ordained state. We see the tenacity of that concept in the Jubilee 2000 debt relief movement promoted by British political economist Martin Dent and supported by the Chancellor of the Exchequer Gordon Brown, who later became England's Prime Minister. For those grown cynical to the possibility of an ancient Scripture contributing towards the breaking of the chains of debt enslavement in the modern world, the Jubilee 2000 movement, though still having achieved only partial success, offers an opportunity to reflect and reconsider!

If ancient Israel had simply adopted the theocratic model in place of the monarchical one without simultaneously radically altering her understanding of the metaphysical basis for human government, the historical developments that made it impossible for the loose confederation of tribes to defend itself against the centralized government and professional armies of the Philistines would have erased Israel from the annals of history. But at this point a remarkable irony enters the picture: The second political model adopted by

Israel was the all too familiar one of monarchy! The irony unfolds in the narrative of 1 Samuel.

The theocratically organized tribal league has come on hard times. The priesthood has fallen into disrepute through the moral turpitude of Eli's sons, the office of judge has been tainted through the corruption of Samuel's sons, and the military has suffered a stinging defeat resulting in the enemy capture of the central symbol of divine presence, the ark of the covenant. Out of these adversities arises the request of the elders: "Give us a king, that we may be like the other nations" (1 Samuel 8:5). Yahweh's consent is not without an accompanying warning: Their king will conscript the young into his court and army, he will levy taxes to support the royal building projects, and finally the warning culminates with the blunt assertion, "you will be his slaves" (8:17).

Given Israel's historical memory of bondage under the Egyptian Pharaoh, the warning of conscription, taxation, and king-sponsored slavery constituted something less than a propitious start for her second form of government. In fact, a few chapters later we find the people confessing to Samuel: "We have added to all our sins the evil of demanding a king for ourselves." Samuel's answer represents one of the most significant contributions to political theory found in the entire Bible. He agrees that they have sinned in asking for a king, but he goes on to assure them of his continuing support through prayer and instruction "in the good and the right way." But there is a very important underlying condition: "Only fear the LORD, and serve him faithfully with all your heart; for consider what great things he has done for you. But if you still do wickedly, you shall be swept away, both you and your king" (1 Samuel 12:24–25). With these words there entered into the history of political reflection for the first time the clear distinction between two levels of government, the level of ultimate authority that belongs solely to God and the level of penultimate, or delegated authority that is the province of human rulers. In the face of this fundamental distinction, differences among diverse government models pale in significance. They will reflect the different conditions pertaining to their place in time and space. From a theological perspective, they are all the products of human sin. Individually, any given regime can claim legitimacy

15

to govern on one basis alone, the extent to which it discharges its divinely authorized responsibility to uphold justice, embody fairness, and maintain peace.

According to the biblical annals, only a handful of kings even approximated these standards, including Asa, Hezekiah, and Josiah. Ultimately, the tensions between the divine standard set for the kings of Israel and the failure of those kings to embody divine righteousness and compassion issued forth in two theologically and politically momentous developments, one lying in the distant future, namely, the concept of a Messiah anointed by God to usher in an age of universal peace and prosperity and one arising with monarchy and ending with monarchy's demise, namely, prophecy. To the latter we now turn, for through the courageous witness of its representatives the oft despised example of God's justice and mercy continued to be proclaimed and through that proclamation the biblical option of rule not by brute force but by gentle compassion survived and found new forms of expression in ages yet unborn.

Prophecy is not a freestanding political model, but one that always assumes the presence of a human regime over against which it provides a standard for critique and restraint. The office of prophet testifies to the fundamental biblical political principle mentioned above, namely, that for the person of faith there is only one ultimate governing authority, God. The prophetic office was charged with the responsibility of representing that authority amidst world governments and human authorities of all types, and the plural is intended here, inasmuch as the prophets spoke on behalf of the universal ruler who was partial to no one regime. Thus Elijah is charged with a message to the Arameans, Amos addresses the treaty violations occurring between the various countries of the eastern Mediterranean, Isaiah identifies Assyria as God's agent in judging Israel, Second Isaiah announces Cyrus the Persian as God's messiah responsible for liberating Israel from her Babylonian captors. But the primary recipient of prophetic address was Israel, including both its rulers and its subjects.

No office in the Bible conveys the seriousness with which the God of Israel takes the political realm more than prophecy. The notion it enlists to depict the essential relation of human government to divine government is political in origin, namely, treaty, or more precisely, covenant. This stresses that human existence on its most fundamental level is relational, and viability for individuals and nations alike is possible solely when two essential relationships are healthy, between the human and God, and between human and human.[14] Moreover, the terms of those parallel relationships are clear, being derived from the nature of the God known to Israel through its history, and spelled out in the Torah. The three pillars of that Torah are worship and mercy and justice. So clear, so universal, so incisive is the moral universe that is upheld by those pillars that it can be captured succinctly in one verse:

> He has told you, O mortal, what is good;
>> and what does the LORD require of you
> but to do justice, and to love kindness,
>> and to walk humbly with your God?" (Micah 6:8)

A consistent theme runs through the Bible regarding the quintessential choice facing humans, both as individuals and as nations. It is summarized in a word of God through Moses in the book of Deuteronomy: "I have set before you life and death . . ." (30:19). This declaration of the irreducible moral structure of the universe at first may sound similar to the moral absolutism expressed by the popular bumper sticker: "The Bible Says It. I believe It. That Settles It." When applied, that approach to the question of biblical authority gives rise to a number of apodictic pronouncements: "The Bible condemns gays. The Bible opposes all forms of abortion. The Bible supports detention of suspected terrorists without the protection of habeas corpus." We must ask, Does this mechanical application of biblical law to contemporary issues capture the true nature of the prophetic message? We need to look more deeply at the prophets, lest we confuse the certainty of God's moral universe with the purported certainties of our own moral biases.

Prophecy first came to expression in opposition to the waxing authority of kings. Nathan rose in opposition to David when the

---

14. In chapter 2 we shall analyze the role that covenant plays in preserving a civilized and humane society, with particular attention to the relation of worship to such essential values as justice, loyalty, and civil harmony.

latter claimed special privileges by virtue of his office. The foreign mercenary whom he sacrificed as an impediment to his claiming the lovely object of his lust, though expendable according to the notion that kings stand above the laws pertaining to subjects, was entitled according to the divine law preserved by the prophets to protection against arbitrary injustice. Unfortunately for Uriah, this protection came to light only posthumously. In similar fashion, Ahab, when he confronted a stubborn subject who refused to surrender his ancestral farmland to the king's desire for a vegetable garden, invoked the age-old ploy of eminent domain and arranged for the execution of the peasant Naboth. But his blatant violation of the higher law predicated on the equal worth of every human life and the entitlement of every family to the benefits of its allotted plot of land led to the convening of the heavenly court, the verdict of which was delivered by the prophetic messenger Elijah. Tragically, the ultimate verdict, like that pronounced by the divine judge in the case of Dietrich Bonhoeffer, Oscar Romero, and Benigno Aquino, was again posthumous. And the long history of the slaughter of righteous individuals who dared to stand up against evil tyrants weighs heavily upon those who seek to understand the nature of divine justice. As perplexing as is the question of theodicy, one thing is clear: All efforts at revising history by ruthless potentates and their defenders have been unable to silence the eternal witness of the martyrs to the ultimate validity of the universal justice of the sole Sovereign and the assured failure of every attempt to supplant God's rule with human alternatives.

Arising from the prophetic tradition's master metaphor of covenant was its favorite genre, the covenant lawsuit. Wherever the prophets witnessed an act of injustice or oppression, they condemned it not in the name of their own moral authority, but in the name of the heavenly Judge, whose court proceedings they faithfully recorded and reported. Take as an example the prophet Hosea, who witnessed blatant immorality, corruption in high circles, and derision of God's sovereignty. He studied the balance of power in the eastern Mediterranean and described how the powerful military force of the Assyrians was poised to destroy a kingdom blind with regard to the consequences of its contempt of the covenant. And the calamity he foresaw was not limited to the geo-political realm, but encompassed the entire created order:

> Hear the word of the LORD, O people of Israel;
>> for the LORD has an indictment against the inhabitants of the land.
> There is no faithfulness or loyalty,
>> and no knowledge of God in the land.
> Swearing, lying, and murder, and stealing and adultery break out;
>> bloodshed follows bloodshed.
> Therefore the land mourns,
>> and all who live in it languish;
> together with the wild animals and the birds of the air,
>> even the fish of the sea are perishing. (Hosea 4:1–3)

Here we see the perspective and role of the prophets. They view reality from the perspective of God's universal moral order, and they announce the consequences of perfidy and repudiation of the commandments, dire consequences for the realm of politics and the world of nature alike.

The second example we cite is the prophet Isaiah. Though he comes from the upper class, he shares the socially sensitive moral vision of his more humble predecessors, Hosea and Amos. His call vision in chapter 6 portrays with brilliant clarity the starting point of every prophetic act or pronouncement, the experience that there is but one ultimate reality in the universe, the Holy One of Israel. It is in the presence of the Holy One that the prophet grasps the nature of divine justice and its singular importance for the durability of societies and nations. The theme that runs throughout Isaiah's prophecy is trust: "In returning and rest you shall be saved; in quietness and in trust shall be your strength" (30:15). Trust in the Holy One means patterning life, as individual and nation, after the divine example. Preeminently it means showing special loving attention to the weak, the ill, the friendless, and the alien. What Isaiah sees instead is "pride": leaders claiming special privileges by merit of their offices, the wealthy exploiting the poor for personal enrichment, the noble class flaunting their items of luxury. Isaiah not only denounces such behavior as immoral; he claims that it is nothing less than a stinging insult to God. A disciple of Isaiah captures with vivid imagery the consequences of such public and national dereliction:

The earth dries up and withers, the world languishes and withers;
    the heavens languish together with the earth.
The earth lies polluted under its inhabitants;
    for they have transgressed laws, violated the statutes,
    broken the everlasting covenant. (Isaiah 24:4–5)

A final arresting example that we shall give from the Hebrew prophets is from Jeremiah:

Woe to him who builds his house by unrighteousness,
    and his upper rooms by injustice;
who makes his neighbors work for nothing
    and does not give them their wages;
who says, "I will build myself a spacious house
    with large upper rooms,
    and who cuts out windows for it,
    paneling it with cedar,
    and painting it with vermilion.
Are you a king
    because you compete in cedar?
Did not your father eat and drink
    and do justice and righteousness?
Then it was well with him.
He judged the cause of the poor and needy;
    then it was well.
Is not this to know me?
    says the Lord. (Jeremiah 22:13–15)

Jeremiah contrasts two views on politics that are as old as the human race, one according to which leaders regard no authority above their own and predicate their policies and rules of conduct on the basis of self-gain, the other according to which all humans are equal in status under one universal, just Ruler, whose example and will they seek to follow. Of course, not only those holding office in political institutions face this basic decision; spiritual leaders do as well, and Jeremiah extends his critique to those who place their trust in the religious institutions to secure their security and well-being: "Do not trust in these deceptive words: 'This is the temple of the LORD, the temple of the LORD, the temple of the LORD'...Will you steal, murder, commit adultery, swear falsely, make offerings to

Baal, and go after other gods . . . and then come and stand before me
in this house . . . and say, 'We are safe'" (7:4, 9–10).

The legacy of the political model of prophecy is profound: It
sets forth the clear distinction between the ultimate authority of
God and the limited, delegated authority of every human government. It defends the equality of every human under God's rule and
bitterly opposes anyone who violates the rights and the irreducible
dignity of subjects, regardless of rank. It vehemently opposes the
invocation of human constructs to lay claim to special divine favor,
whether nation, cult, or social status. "Chosenness" in the Bible is a
call to special responsibility, not special privilege. Amos took direct
aim at the boasting of the people of Israel that their historical roots
in the exodus provided proof positive that they were God's favored
nation:

> Are you not like the Ethiopians to me,
>   O people of Israel, says the LORD.
> Did I not bring Israel up from the land of Egypt,
>   and the Philistines from Caphtor and the Arameans from Kir?
> (Amos 9:7)

Any person of faith today who takes seriously the bearing of
the Bible on society and world affairs will sit humbly and attentively
at the feet of the prophets.

There remain three other political models in the Old Testament,
each in turn leaving an important legacy for those seeking to understand the meaning of biblical faith for contemporary society and
politics. Here we can only mention each of them briefly.

The sapiential model draws not upon the specific stories and
laws of Israel's history, but upon what amounts to an empirical study
of the natural order. This is the reason the book of Proverbs, for example, does not infer rules for life from the Exodus or Mount Sinai,
but rather from the patterns observed in the life of wise and foolish
humans, from the behavior of ants and beasts, and from the forces
of nature and the ordering of the heavens. Human institutions, like
ethical norms, are regarded as parts of a universal order, and it is
perhaps not surprising that submission to the authority of kings and

judges rather than radical critique of existing social structures is the preferred style of sapiential politics. Consider Proverbs 24:21–22:

> My child, fear the LORD and the king,
>> And do not become involved with those who seek change;
> For disaster comes from them suddenly,
>> And who knows the ruin that both can bring?

Since many of the sapiential writings are tied to a royal court setting, it follows that a close connection is displayed between civil order and a strong monarchy with the king benefiting from a sizeable bureaucracy:

> Where there is no guidance, a nation falls,
>> but in the abundance of counselors there is safety.
> (Proverbs 11:14)

It would be a mistake, though, to conclude that the sages of the wisdom literature give blind assent to royal authority. Kings are authorized to rule by God, and their success and the happiness of their people depend on their embodying divine justice in their decrees and judgments. Though they are to enjoy the loyalty of their subjects, they themselves must submit to the laws of the Creator. It is thus accurate to say that the fundamental principle of biblical politics, the subordination of the penultimate authority of human leaders to the ultimate authority of God, remains intact in the sapiential writings of the Old Testament, as it still does in the description of governing authority in the New Testament by the Apostle Paul: "Let every person be subject to the ruling authorities; for there is no authority except from God, and those authorities that exist have been instituted by God" (Romans 13:1).

Rulers and judges are to study the writings of the sages of old as a source of wisdom and discernment, on the basis of which they are to provide a clear vision for their subordinates and subjects. We read from Sirach 10:1–3:

> A wise magistrate educates his people,
>> and the rule of an intelligent person is well ordered.
> As the people's judge is, so are his officials;
>> as the ruler of the city is, so are all its inhabitants.

> An undisciplined king ruins his people,
> > but a city becomes fit to live in
> > through the understanding of its rulers.

What is more, the emphasis of the prophets on even-handed justice and advocacy for the poor is not neglected by the sages, as is evidenced by Proverbs 31:8–9:

> Speak out for those who cannot speak,
> > for the rights of all the destitute.
> Speak out, judge righteously,
> > defend the rights of the poor and needy.

In general, the contribution of the sapiential tradition to biblical politics is insufficiently appreciated. Few scholars (notable in this regard are James Barr and James L. Crenshaw) have pointed to the importance of the wisdom writings in a comprehensive understanding of biblical theology. Within contemporary thought, these writings remind us of the importance of rigorous intellectual scrutiny as a restraint on sectarian fanaticism and parochial bias. It would be difficult to conceive of the process that led to the composition of the founding documents of the United States without the presence of the sage advice of Benjamin Franklin and James Madison, thinkers steeped in eighteenth-century equivalents of the biblical sapiential tradition, namely, English Deism and French philosophy. We have also noted how Nelson Mandela, while acknowledging his indebtedness to prophetic tradition, also drew freely on pre-Christian tribal custom, thereby exercising the openness of one who could recognize divine truth beyond the borders of explicitly Christian culture.

Closely related to the sapiential model, though at the same time distinct from it because of its explicitly Jewish orientation, is the *accommodationalist* model that we associate with Ezra and Nehemiah. It grew out of the Jewish experience during the Second Temple period of living no longer as an independent nation able to address the relation of religion and politics free from outside intervention, but as a vassal state under the firm control of the Persians. It amounted to the working out of a compromise that conformed to the imperial conditions of a foreign occupier at the same time as it permitted the Jews to remain faithful to their Torah and their native customs. This model became vitally important in subsequent ages of Judaism, for not only in the Persian period, but during the Hellenistic and Roman periods and on into the Middle Ages the Jewish communities in the Diaspora were obliged to continue to adjust their lives to the hegemony of foreign rulers. And when it comes to the question of the legacy of Ezra's model for contemporary theo-political reflection, we do well to consider John Howard Yoder's suggestion that for the Christian who would be true to the politics of Jesus and Paul, the Jewish diaspora model can serve as a chastening corrective to the Constantinian model of Christian imperialism.[15]

The sixth political model found in the Bible is the *apocalyptic* model. It arises as an adaptation of prophetic faith to the bleak setting of persecution where the faithful suffer at the hands either of their own compatriots or foreign adversaries. The floruit of apocalyptic politics occurred between the second century BCE and the end of the second century CE, and its literary expressions in the Bible are most notably Daniel and the book of Revelation. This political model has been of vital importance in modern times for Christian communities suffering under religious persecution, such as Jewish communities and the Confessing Church in Nazi Germany. It gives expression to the central confession of biblical politics, namely, that there is but one ultimate Ruler of the universe and that no human ruler has the right to demand the unqualified allegiance of his subjects. It upholds the belief that in the final verdict, the moral structure of the universe will be maintained and all those who have been sentenced unjustly in world courts will be vindicated in the divine court of justice. The visions of the apocalyptic writings depict God's final victory over all opposition and function to preserve the hope of the faithful, even in the face of a world that seems to have come under the control of the Evil One and its hosts.

For the majority of Christians in the world today who enjoy the protection of freedom of belief under the laws of their states, apocalyptic politics is not as politically relevant as the prophetic

15. See Yoder, *The Politics of Jesus.*

model, inasmuch as their situation allows them to seek to reform their societies on the basis of God's rule of justice and mercy. In other words, the temporary withdrawal from political engagement provided by the apocalyptic model would be inappropriate. It is within such settings that the Christian must scrutinize the arbitrary application of apocalyptic politics by such sensationalist authors as Hal Lindsay and Timothy LaHay. To demonstrate that their sectarian, death-wish theology is heretical would require more time than we have at present.[16]

Equally impossible would be the next important step, namely, a discussion of the politics of the New Testament, for it should be obvious that for Christians, the vital lessons of the six Old Testament models are mediated to us through the politics of Jesus and the apostles.

Here we must limit our observations regarding the vast topic of politics in the New Testament to a few essentials. First, it is as important to understand the background of these writings in the Roman Empire as it was to understand the various historical settings of the Old Testament within a world dominated in turn by Egypt, Assyria, Babylonia and Persia, for the dynamic historical understanding that began with the exodus continues into New Testament times, as does the fundamental belief that there is but one absolute Ruler of the universe before whom this world's potentates are mere passing shadows. What this means is that political strategies will continue to avoid static imposition of a timeless blueprint and instead justify political positions on the basis of the criterion of their adequacy in representing God's governance of justice and mercy within specific historical and geographical settings.

In the case of Jesus portrayed in the Gospels, we find a politics of critical engagement with the Roman and Jewish leaders, and the uncompromising insistence on the sole Lordship of the heavenly Father. Since the courageous witness of Jesus threatened both the Roman control of a rebellious, sprawling empire and the Jewish leaders deadly fear of any movement that could become the catalyst of revolt, it was unavoidable that Jesus took his place in the line of witnesses to God's sovereignty whom the rulers of this world sought

16. Cf. Hanson, *Old Testament Apocalyptic*.

to silence. The centrality for faith of this particular martyr lies in the fact that vindication of the bearer of divine justice and mercy came on the third day after his crucifixion, and thus established like never before for the faithful the basis for their vocation of bearing witness in the world to the only ultimate government, God's government and the reign of his Son.

Jesus' political position embodied the dialectic of God's ultimate ruling authority and the derived, penultimate rule of humans. Let us consider two examples from the Gospels.

In relation to the Roman emperor, the classic formulation is "Render to Caesar what is Caesar's and to God what is God's" (Matthew 22:15–22 // Mark 12:13–17 // Luke 20:20–26). Against the background of the politics of the entire Bible, believers then and now hear what the Romans would not have heard, namely, that everything is ultimately God's, and therefore what will be rendered to Caesar will be what God has delegated to earthly rulers. Added to this is the defining qualification that their legitimacy remains intact only to the extent that they promote the universal justice and mercy of God.

Since divine justice and mercy were more often violated than upheld by the Romans, the question of fitting response was especially difficult for Jesus and his followers. Enormous pressure was placed on them to follow the path of the Zealots and the Sicarii of open revolt. But it is clear that Jesus regarded such a suicide tactic as a form of idolatry, that is, placing nationalistic goals over the purposes of God's kingdom. Patience and suffering constituted the truthful path to "thy kingdom come, thy will be done, on earth as it is in heaven."

In relation to the claim that religious institutions and authorities hold over those who have submitted to the rule of God, the classic story revolves around the half-shekel temple tax (Matthew 17:24–27). Should the disciples pay it, and thereby acknowledge the authority over them of the temple administrators, or should they assert their true spiritual citizenship by refusing to pay, thereby raising the specter of violence? The path of submission placed in jeopardy their sole allegiance to God. But violence was not the way to the Kingdom taught by their Lord. The story has an ending that exquisitely upholds the dialectic of biblical politics: Not the disciples, but a fish pays the temple tax! Covenant fidelity and political pragmatism are simultaneously commended through a story that like Aesop's fables proves that animals often are our most subtle teachers!

The political position of the Apostle Paul is even more complex, and many fine monographs in recent years have challenged older assumptions.[17] At the heart of the controversy is Romans 13, a key chapter, which we above suggested is related to the accommodationist model and should perhaps be understood in relation to Paul's later writings, especially those written from Roman prisons. At any rate, it is important to recognize that the fundamental biblical principle of God's sole authority is affirmed in the leading verse of Paul's discourse, "for there is no authority except from God." That having been said, the fact remains that in Romans 13, Paul seems to be more accommodating than either Jesus of the Gospels or even Paul himself in many of his other pronouncements. A plausible explanation for this is that he is being extraordinarily careful not to exacerbate the growing tensions between the Romans, the Jews, and the growing Jesus movement. Also not to be forgotten is Paul's education under the Pharisees, which would explain the resonances between his thought and the earlier position of Ezra in relation to the Persians.

A third political position is staked out by the book of Revelation. Christian communities throughout the Empire were being sacrificed to the wrath of Nero and Diocletian. Powerless before this overwhelming power, they interpret it as the Anti-Christ. They find refuge in the message of final vindication after death and accordingly adopt the strategy of the apocalyptic political model. Again the dynamic flexibility of biblical politics to changing conditions is in evidence, providing an invaluable source of hope and strategy for survival in modern times for Christian leaders like Dietrich Bonhoeffer and Hans Lilje as they encountered yet again the face of the Anti-Christ in Adolf Hitler and his collaborators. And in our own time, the poignancy of the apocalyptic message has become apparent as the specter of genocide continues to cast its ghastly pall over Ruwanda, the Congo, and Sudan.

17. Cassidy, *Paul in Chains*, for example.

THE CONTRIBUTION OF THE BIBLE TO CONTEMPORARY POLITICS

The diverse and often contradictory conclusions that individuals and communities draw from the Bible regarding the controversial issues of contemporary life represent one of the areas of religion that attracts the most attention in the popular media. To the "cultural despisers of Christianity," the utter lack of unanimity among religious people offers occasion for ridicule or disdainful dismissal. For religious zealots, conflict is welcomed as a sign of the approach of the climactic skirmish that will determine the winners in the "battle for the Bible." On the other hand, for many conscientious people of faith who want to do the right thing in relation to issues such as human sexuality and world peace, the fact that not only individual believers but entire denominations seem to be locked in intractable dispute over important moral issues is a source of great distress.

It is especially to such people that we now turn to reflect on the important issue of the essential nature of the theory of interpretation one uses as a guide to discerning the contemporary meaning of Scripture, which is to say, the issue of hermeneutics. It may be helpful to bring to light the presuppositional starting point of the two positions into which, in the most general sense, most interpretative strategies seeking to define biblical authority fall.

We begin with the approach that can be called absolutist. Proponents of this position within Christianity and Islam commonly go by the label "fundamentalist," whereas within Judaism "ultra-orthodox" is the term most commonly used. All three ascribe to the words of Scripture (and in Judaism to the total corpus of words attributed to Moses) the attribute of truth transcending the limits of historical particularity and the fallibility of human understanding. In this approach, human participation in revelatory events is reduced to the formal matter of transmission, meaning that the words of the Quran are the words of Allah mediated by the Prophet Mohammed, the words of Christian Scripture (in the original transcripts) are the words of God inerrantly recorded by human authors, and the Hebrew Bible, Mishnah and Talmud are the words Moses received from God on Mt. Sinai.

In the case of the Christian version of absolutism, the assumption of inerrant Scripture is accompanied by the belief that the Bible contains answers to all matters of belief and morals if read literally and without the biases imposed by liberal interpreters deriving not from the realm of divine revelation but from the human realm of rationalist philosophy and secular bias. Biblical truth is thereby insulated from the limits endemic to human existence and the flux characteristic of history. Through literal reading, the plain truth of the Bible becomes clear regarding homosexuality and abortion. And depending on the particular interpreter, the list can go on to include global issues like the return of all Jews to Israel and even eschatological matters like the date of the end of the world.

Commonly, the critique of the absolutist hermeneutic begins with the marshalling of evidence intended to discredit the notion of inerrancy, such as the presence of two creation stories, conflicting accounts of a single historical event, and misattribution of a quotation. That starting point is unfortunate, inasmuch as its negativity seems indistinguishable from the scorn of the cultural despiser and, more importantly, it fails to place front and center the powerful positive argument for the alternative position.

Let our criticism be stated clearly: The absolutist position rests on an unbiblical concept of divine revelation! In the Bible, God is not presented as an aloof lecturer who occasionally breaks his customary austere silence with a solemn pronouncement of abstract truth directed to Moses or Isaiah or the Apostle Paul, humans viewed as passive amanuensises who take up chisel or stylus or pen and meticulously record the dictated words. Rather, God is encountered in the raw stuff of human experience such as the dread moment when fleeing slaves tremble as a crushing army of the Pharaoh descends upon them to drag them back into captivity, and what will become a passage in Scripture arises as their joyous response to seeing calamity transformed into deliverance: "The LORD is my strength and my might, and he has become my salvation" (Exodus 15:2). And the hand of God is recognized by an anonymous prophet of the Exile as he observes the Persian Emperor Cyrus breaking the fist of the Babylonians and preparing the way for the return of the Jews to their beloved homeland: "For the sake of my servant

Jacob, and Israel my chosen, I call you by your name, I surname you, though you do not know me" (Isaiah 45:4). Scripture is written when they respond to a miraculous deliverance in a hymn of praise (Isaiah 45:25). Revelation in this understanding is not the mechanical transmission of abstract truths, but the discovery of Immanuel, God with us, in the joys and tragedies of human existence. The Bible consists not of words frozen in eternity, but testimonies by a living faith community of their awareness of living not alone but in the ever-watchful presence of a loving God. The Word of God is not a set of propositions trumping human experience and excluding the ongoing exercise of discernment of that loving God in the here and now, but rather the framework of an ongoing conversation between a God continuing to create and to redeem and a people attentive to God's presence in their midst. Part of the beauty of this historical understanding of the origin of Scripture and its ongoing interpretation in the community of faith is its congruity with central tenets of classical biblical faith, for example, *covenant* as relationship between humans and a God who chooses to enlist partners in his activity on behalf of fullness of life for all, and *incarnation* as God's entering into intimate proximity with humanity not in the form of disembodied spirit but real flesh and blood. What is being affirmed in this description is the incarnate Bible of Luther and Calvin, described by the former as "a worm of a book" and the latter as "God's stuttering," powerful metaphors intended to stress the genuinely human dimension of Scripture.

Though it is far preferable to present the alternative to absolutism in positive terms such as the preceding, candor also leads us to note that the notion of an inerrant Bible resembles in an essential respect the timeless myths that defined the relation of ancient peoples like the Egyptians and the Babylonians to their deities. Unlike the epic of the Israelites, which we have described as arising out of historical experience and inviting ongoing development first through the stages of growth leading to canon and then through lively reinterpretation, the myths of Israel's ancient neighbors depicted eternal realities in the realm of the gods that were mediated through scribal specialists to their particular cultures as a timeless template for the ordering of their religious cult, political institutions, and cultural mores. By repudiating myth, ancient Israel created room for all humans to experience dignity as equals before a God who related to them as one respecting their freedom and their right to accept or reject his beneficence. Such freedom involves far greater ambiguity and risk than the certainty offered by a timeless myth, but according to biblical faith, such freedom is the *sine qua non* of creatures created in the image of God. And it is within the context of that freedom that individuals and communities of faith today consult the living Word of God in the effort to be obedient and productive children of God.[18]

How does that obedience and productivity translate into citizenship? How can Christians enrich discussions in the public square by drawing on the riches of their scriptural tradition while still being respectful of the broad diversity of religious and moral perspectives within their society?

People of faith can view their civic involvement as an aspect of participating in the unfolding epic of God's ongoing creation dedicated to the restoration to health of an order in which creatures large and small have been fractured and alienated from one another and in which even the inanimate world has been degraded.

18. It must be emphasized that the distinction between historical and mythical language in the Bible is not rigid. For biblical poets and storytellers and historians to renounce mythic images as part of their repertory would be tantamount with modern writers eschewing all allusions to symbolic imagery or flights into fantasy. The poets who composed Exodus 15 and Judges 5 were impelled by their experiences to allow mundane historical experiences to invade the mythic classics that gave structure to ancient societies. And later writers like the exilic Isaiah and Job with equal license channeled the powerful images of theogonic and cosmogonic myth into the historical themes that constituted the epic of the people Israel. Such flexibility in the interplay of mythic and historical motifs in the biblical writings underscores the dynamism of political thought in the Bible. The God of the Bible was not viewed as setting up one single form of human government locked in place in a celestially derived perfection for all times and places. The authors and tridents that gave shape to the "Law of the King" in Deuteronomy 17 and prophets like Amos and Isaiah stood in opposition to priests and kings who laid claim to prerogatives that belonged exclusively to God. They regarded any appeal to eternal paradigms as warrants for the absolute authority of kings and priests as an assault on the freedom of the only authority they were willing to acknowledge as ultimate.

As free citizens of God's reign of restorative justice and all-inclusive compassion, Christians are commissioned to be ambassadors of the New Creation through which God seeks to restore the entire cosmos to wholeness (2 Corinthians 5:16–21 and Romans 8:18–39). Though they view participation in government as an important part of their discipleship, their mode of engagement differs from zealots seeking to impose their theocratic visions on a godless order. Precisely because they regard all human institutions as imperfect and provisional and recognize the wisdom of those adhering to different views of the world, they accept the debate and compromise involved in policy-making as a natural part of laboring for the healing of the present order even as they yearn for the permanent and perfect peace that only God can inaugurate.

In our political engagement, we are deployed not with a timeless blueprint in hand, but with the example of ancestors in the faith who responded to the call to covenant partnership in an ever-changing world. Inspired by Abraham, we dare to move beyond comfortable boundaries, with Moses we dare speak God's word of truth to tyrannical power, and like Amos we embrace as our strategy doing justice, loving kindness, and walking humbly with our God (Amos 6:8). Reformed theologian Paul Lehman contrasted the absolutist political philosophy of fundamentalism with the legacy of the Reformation, which legacy, in his words, introduced "a liberating grasp of the ways of God with men and thus also the possibility of ever fresh and experimental responses to the dynamics and the humanizing character of the divine activity in the world. This meant for ethics the displacement of the prescriptive and absolute formulation of its claims by the contextual understanding of what God is doing in the world to make and to keep human life human."[19]

Application of this dynamic understanding of God's redemptive presence in the world to political process leads to this conclusion: The specific form that the branches of a particular government should take is to arise from the diligent search of the citizenry for the structures most suitable for upholding mercy and justice within the concreteness of its global setting and its temporal location

19. Lehman, *Ethics in a Christian Context*, 14.

within an every changing and challenging world. This conclusion derives from a central tenet of the Christian faith, namely, that human governments are legitimate only to the extent that they serve the purposes of even-handed justice, provision for the needs of the poor and infirm, and global peace. It is solely from the promotion of these purposes that human institutions derive their authority to rule.

From this understanding the church derives these principles regarding its responsibility vis-à-vis society and government:

1. The perspective from which social and political issues will be viewed is its carefully delineated vision of God's universal reign.

2. The responsibility of the church to government will take the form of representation of and advocacy for God's Reign.

3. Its mode of action will include, as appropriate, critique, admonition, and support, uncompromised by penultimate claims such as patriotism and ecclesiastical loyalty, but respectful of the constitutional principles of a legitimately constituted host state.

Even after these principles are clear, an important practical question remains: With sensitivity to its particular location in time and place, how does a given community of faith go about the task of enriching political process with the specific wisdom and insight into truth derived from its own tradition while remaining respectful of participants from other religious and philosophical perspectives? What form of discourse will be faithful, legal, fair, and effective, given the wide diversity of religious and nonreligious perspectives present in a pluralistic society? A lively debate rages over this question, with three major alternatives being offered by scholars variously trained in philosophy, political science, and theology. The three alternatives are these:

1. *Political liberalism*: John Rawls has proposed that public discourse in a modern, religiously diverse society must be confined to arguments comprehensible to all participants, thus excluding appeal to comprehensive worldviews, such as reli-

gion, for warrants that will make sense only to adherents.[20] He later modified this by conceding that religious warrants could be admitted into public discussion, but they carried no weight if not backed up with rational justifications, a modification emotively significant but without philosophical substance.[21] Richard Rorty argues along similar lines, except that his reason is more pragmatically than philosophically based, namely, the introduction of religious language in political discussions amounts to a "conversation stopper."[22]

2. *Communitarianism*. Stanley Hauerwas, drawing on Alasdair MacIntyre,[23] argues that political liberalism has impoverished public moral discourse by depriving it of the depth dimension of faith, that is, the dimension that provides people and movements with moral motivation and specific ethical content. The attempt to find a neutral language not only reduces public debate to drabness but privileges rationalism over other alternatives.[24]

3. *Pragmatism*. Jeffrey Stout suggests that public discourse should be pragmatically goal-oriented, with all perspectives—religious and nonreligious—welcomed, granted that they abide by the rules of civility and remain focused on and mutually committed to the qualities that constitute a good society.[25]

In the efforts of the church to translate biblical truth into political process, the above three alternatives will challenge thought and provide important insights. In the final analysis, however, a theo-political hermeneutic is required that is simultaneously true to Christian beliefs and moral principles and suitable for the political settings within which we live. Rather than choosing between political liberalism, communitarianism, and pragmatism, such a

20. Rawls, *A Theory of Justice*.

21. Rawls, *Political Liberalism*.

22. Rorty, "Religion as Conversation-stopper."

23. MacIntyre, *After Virtue*.

24. Hauerwas, *Performing the Faith*.

25. Stout, *Democracy and Tradition*. Cf. Thiemann, *Religion in Public Life*.

hermeneutic can draw judiciously from all three in the process of forging a strategy that strikes the delicate balance between confessional integrity and civility.

A FIVE-STEP HERMENEUTIC FOR A BIBLICAL BASED POLITICAL THEOLOGY

We have offered examples of the dangers inherent in an undisciplined application of biblical verses, motifs, and themes to contemporary domestic and international issues. We also have given an overview of the political models that arose over the course of biblical history by means of which our spiritual ancestors sought to relate their faith to the political, economic, and social realities within which they lived. The picture that emerged was not of a static blueprint for relating religion to politics, but rather a dynamic one characterized by adaptability to ever changing circumstances, both within the nation and in neighboring empires often led by imperious rulers. The nature of the biblical sources themselves thus deprives us of the simple exercise of consulting an authoritative manual for answers to all problems. Not timeless answers, but testimony to a living God involved with his creation and the people responding to his call to partnership on behalf of fullness of life for all, such is the authority to which we have fallen heir.

The hermeneutic that grows out of this understanding of the Bible will take the form of a process rather than a mechanical deductive exercise, a process conducted not by an elite cadre of experts but by a faith community embracing people from all lands and from all social and economic classes and races, a community moreover that works cooperatively with justice-loving members of all other communities. The following brief description of a five step hermeneutic will offer a glimpse into my understanding of the interpretive process in which a faith community engages as it turns to the Bible for guidance from the perspective of the Christian faith and within the context of a society characterized by broad religious and philosophical diversity and a history of a lively legal and legislative debate over the issue of the proper relationship between church and state.

First, if we believe that the cornerstone of a Christian political theology is the distinction between God's ultimate authority and the derived, penultimate authority of every human institution, we must abide in a living relationship with that God, whom we know personally through his Son, the Messiah who has inaugurated God's reign, and by whose Spirit we are supported through every trial. Where the triune God is most intimately present to us is in worship, where we are invited to celebrate the Kingdom-to-come that is already present through participation in the Eucharist and where we hear anew the Word that directs our lives. We can formulate this first stage of our hermeneutic thus: The starting point of authentic Christian political reflection and action is worship, for there it is that we experience the living God awakening our conscience, kindling our compassion, and directing our actions on behalf of justice and advocacy for the suffering and the poor. Lest we be tempted into seeing the Church as just one more social action movement, we can restate the first step in our theo-political hermeneutic thus: worship is the most political thing the community of faith does.

Secondly, it stands to reason that we must be adequately tutored in our biblical and confessional traditions to be informed and reliable contributors to the public forum of the bearing of our scriptural legacy on contemporary realities. It may be helpful to note that on these first two levels, the communitarian position can contribute enormously to clarification of the convictions and moral principles to which the faith community must bear witness if it is to remain faithful to its prophetic calling. For as Stanley Hauerwas has emphasized repeatedly, to adopt the latitudinarianism of liberals like John Rawls dulls both the specific message of the Gospel to world affairs and threatens to cut off the ambassadors of the Gospel from the source of their passion for justice and mercy, the God who in Christ stands in solidarity with every individual impoverished by corrupt economic structures and oppressed by tyrannical political authorities.

Thirdly, we must cultivate the skill to translate the moral principles we derive from our faith into reasonable discourse that is comprehensible to all fair-minded citizens and is free of special pleading. It is at this stage that it becomes apparent that one must go beyond communitarianism if one is to fashion a theo-political hermeneutic adequate for a religiously diverse society and world. And it is not only the contemporary world that prods one towards a broader vision of political partnerships. The primary incentive comes from the testimony of the Jewish and Christian Scriptures that God is the Sovereign of all nations and that our spiritual ancestors in the Bible and subsequent history often drew insight from the religious and moral insights of other cultures. While recognizing that the inner-faith community struggle to gain clarity on the guidance provided by Scripture for contemporary issues is a richly communitarian endeavor, the search for tactics that can guide the move from the parochialism of specific faith community to the thickness and messiness of political debate reaches beyond communitarianism. The participation called for is tempered by John Rawls's vision of a democratic society in which the rights of liberty and equality are secured for all citizens and in which justice is defined broadly by being grounded in warrants accessible to the scrutiny of all reasonable citizens. Supplementing this liberal position, however, is the important qualification provided by Jeffrey Stout's pragmatism: The arguments allowed to enter the public debate over the principles of the good society such as liberty, equality, and justice are not to exclude religiously grounded arguments, for to do so would be to prejudice the case by exempting rationalism from the excluded category of comprehensive doctrines. Rather, Stout argues, insights derived from comprehensive doctrines, including religious ones, are to be welcomed, with the condition that their protagonists must commit themselves to the kind of civil etiquette that pledges respectful attention to differing religious points of view and dedication to forging policy and initiating action that leads to the improvement of life for all members of society (and ultimately, of the world).

Fourthly, participants in the public debate who view their role not as proponents of their own exclusive theocratic vision but as obedient servants of the God of all peoples will be capable of listening attentively to viewpoints arising from other religious and ethical groups as a means of enriching their own understanding. Awareness of the limitations of any individual's or community's grasp of complex aspects of modern society and world leads to an openness to cooperation with others and a pragmatic spirit willing to work with political alliances sharing the awareness that while "perfect" political institutions and social structures are the illusory constructs of absolutists, concrete progress can be made in improving the quality of life of all citizens in areas such as quality education, universal health care, and equal opportunities in the workplace. In joining broad-based coalitions, participants will not set aside their specific, confessionally, and scripturally based identity, but will continue to be oriented by the moral compass that identity provides. At the same time they will enthusiastically encourage participants from other traditions to remain equally aware of and true to their systems of belief and morals, for to them cooperation reaching across religious boundaries does not entail exclusion, but mutual enrichment through honest and civil debate. To the satisfaction of witnessing the progress that such inter-faith cooperation can accomplish comes another benefit: We will return to the communitarian debates of our own congregations (Step 2) chastened regarding certain aspects of our limited understandings and enriched by the contributions of other communities to our shared humanity and moral discernment.

Fifthly, the courage, steadiness, patience, and gracefulness with which we engage in the challenging task of building a more humane society and peaceful world are attributable to no personal virtue or privileged institutional investiture, but to the moral qualities that are the fruits of our living between spiritual bookends: worship, which we have already described as our source, and the eschatological Reign of God, which is our goal. The importance of eschatological hope as a living part of our consciousness is illustrated best by the lives of the martyrs. Most vividly preserved in our memory perhaps is Dietrich Bonhoeffer, who had numerous opportunities to take a path that would have enabled him to escape from the Nazis, indeed a path that would have been respected and admired by all of his co-workers, but who did not waver from following the path of discipleship that led to the gallows set up by an absolutist regime that could not tolerate the challenge to its authority by a prophet. It is no accident that in modern times no theologian of the Church has provided a deeper insight into the politics of the Kingdom than Bonhoeffer, for in his own following the way of Christ he etched into modern consciousness the distinction between empty victories built on worldly power and eternal victory arising out of brokenness and death. To Bonhoeffer, no adversary, whether Hitler or his own personal doubts, could crush him, for he was sustained by Christ's promise of the Kingdom's ultimate triumph (Revelation 11:15).

It remains to show by way of a concrete example how one central confession from our biblical heritage can be translated into constructive public discourse, that confession being the first commandment: "I am the Lord your God, who brought you out of the land of Egypt, out of the house of slavery; you shall have no other gods before me" (Exodus 20:2–3).

While this is a confession specific to one religious tradition that will not be shared by all participants in the wider context of public debate, the notion that no human institution can place unconditional claims on the conscience of the individual certainly will find support in many quarters of society. While our particular faith will give depth to our support of the notion of the inalienable rights of liberty and equality of the individual by pointing to a God who, by transcending all that is human, relativizes all claims made by human authorities, our public articulation of that notion will reach beyond the communitarian language of our Scripture and confessions. Let us identify several directions in which we can move from the intrinsic universal truth residing in the first commandment.

For one, we can help create an alternative to a view of economics that is driven strictly by the notion of the autonomy of the marketplace. We can argue that that view must be subject to critique deriving from the more universal notions of equality and shared human dignity, notions buttressed both by the philosophical traditions upon which the founding documents of the United States were based and by the biblical values to which the Founders simultaneously subscribed. Unbridled *liaise faire* economic policy is thus exposed to a double critique in which secular humanitarians and compassionate people of faith become partners rather than rivals: How can an individual enjoy the right to liberty if the unbridled forces of the market hold him or her in the bondage of impoverishment?

The same principle of the relativization of all human ideologies and theories will apply when we denounce the subsuming of educational and health care priorities to tax cuts aimed at increasing the competitive edge of corporations through the concentration of capital among venture capitalists and those applying advanced methods of leveraging and arbitrage. Concentration of capital is not an end in itself, and indeed, among competing values, it can be argued that priority status given to a financial commitment to education with the aim of "leaving no child behind" is a vastly more productive policy than unalloyed supply-side economics, a position again that can be cogently argued from the depths of our confessional commitment to the God of every individual in terms that are entirely suitable for a style of public discourse committed to civility and equal access to all participants.

A similar understanding of the positive role of religious perspectives within the context of public debate relates to the debate over two definitions of the rights guaranteed by the U.S. Constitution, namely, a positive definition and a negative (or "procedural") definition. Which definition is the more defensible? Increasingly, as pointed out by Michael Sandel, the U.S. has been cultivating the case for negative rights, that is, the individual is entitled to the broad latitude of rights limited only at the point of avoiding violation of the equally broadly understood rights of other citizens. How different the issue of rights becomes when the more classical republican (i.e., positive) definition of rights embraces all that enables the individual to realize his or her full potential as a human being. Suddenly, government support of universal health, open access to job opportunities, and equal educational opportunities for all become important aspects of constitutional responsibility. And once again, the implication for the faith communities is clear: Their particular scriptural and confessional traditions can be introduced into public debates that invite such participation. All that is required is what we earlier articulated as proper etiquette: a civil style of open debate and a defense of the right of other world-views to represent their perspectives that is as explicit as the defense of one's own participation.

We could proceed similarly in relation to international conflict and the prioritizing of human, rather than economic, benefits and costs in policies relating to debt relief, energy policy, and conflict resolution. But following a list of examples that for many will be perceived to reflect a "tilt to the left," it is essential to emphasize that equally important are themes kept alive by religious conservatives such as personal morality and individual integrity, honesty in the discharge of public duty, leadership that provides examples of virtue and compassion, and family values. In these realms as well faith informed insights can engage other perspectives in a manner that is at once frank and civil.

Having opened up some of the issues confronted by the individual and community committed to relating biblical beliefs and values to contemporary issues, we prepare ourselves best for further probes into specific issues regarding the Bible and politics by reconnecting with our compass provided by our Lord's prayer: "thy kingdom come, thy will be done, on earth as it is in heaven."

2 Worship—Touchstone of Christian Political Action

Many conscientious, modern-day Christians experience a sense of perplexity, if not futility, when they survey their nation and world and ask what their faith requires of them in relation both to domestic and international issues. They witness conflicting approaches among national leaders to pressing needs such as health care for all citizens that is accessible and affordable, high quality education for the young, regardless of the economic status of their parents or geographical location of their homes, and protection from financial institutions that place profit above service and seem willing to compromise ethical standards. All too often they witness leaders they have entrusted with the well-being of all citizens becoming mired in conflicts-of-interest, fraud, and moral turpitude. In viewing a wider world suffering from staggering inequities in wealth distribution, political instability bordering on anarchy, and the ever-looming cloud of terrorism, they experience a sense of helplessness. What can the individual believer or faith community do to address such enormous and complex issues in a meaningful way that can contribute to a more just society and peaceable world.

In the previous chapter we outlined an approach to the interpretation and application of the Bible that maintains a balance between prophetic critique based on the specific confessions and ethical principles of the Christian faith and civility within an increasingly diverse citizenry. In this chapter we turn to insights gleaned from political science and social ethics to enhance our understanding of the responsibilities carried by one who believes that God has created all creatures and that God wills for all humans living conditions that enable realization of their full human potential and for the nations of the world economic conditions that promote peace, mutual cooperation and respect. Our guide will be the American theologian and social ethicist, H. Richard Niebuhr, who through his courageous integration of the central beliefs and moral principles of the Christian faith into a profound understanding of both human nature and human behavior as it takes shape in human societies not only emerged as one of the most influential religious leaders of the twentieth century but continues to speak with prophetic clarity to the issues of our day.

Viewing his world in the aftermath of the devastation of World War II, Niebuhr observed that the democracies that had survived the assault of totalitarianism remained, nevertheless, in very deep trouble from within. Though he died nearly a half-century ago, one theme in his writings still speaks with remarkable poignancy to a central defect in the ethical framework within which business and politics are conducted and to which scandals on Wall Street and financial turmoil in the banking and housing markets can be traced. It was his claim that a root cause of the decline of democracy was the loss of the qualities inherent in "covenant," qualities that had played a key role in the development of the structures of commerce, law, and government over the course of several centuries, qualities without which unswerving commitment to the common good on the part of citizens collapsed into individualistic pursuits and partisan conflicts. With the loss of those qualities, a world was laid vulnerable to ravages of selfishness and greed.

It was not Niebuhr's claim that contemporary government and commerce operate entirely without the benefit of structural models defining the obligations of involved parties. Rather, what he chronicled was the qualitative change that occurred when covenant, within which parties consented to truth-telling and honoring of obligations as an unconditional and unlimited commitment under God, was replaced by contract, understood as an agreement between parties designed to serve their rights and self-interests and carrying a provision for annulment at the behest of one or both of the parties.[1]

---

1. The climate in which covenant would yield to contract as the dominant model of regulating contractual arrangements was the Enlightenment, a climate in which the center of the universe switched from God to the human agent. For the classic formulation of social contract, see Locke, *Two Treatises of Government* (1690).

"Contract always implies limited, covenant unlimited commitment; contract is entered into for the sake of mutual advantages; covenant implies the presence of a cause to which all advantages may need to be sacrificed."[2]

Though Michael Sandel does not refer to H. Richard Niebuhr in his 1996 book *Democracy's Discontent*, his central argument dovetails nicely with Niebuhr's central thesis.[3] He believes that something was lost when a nation moved away from republican political theory and practice, with its emphasis on commitment of citizens to the common good and the concomitant need for the cultivation of civic virtue, to a procedural democracy, in which the protection of the rights of individuals became government's paramount responsibility, and particular positions on moral and religious issues were restricted to the personal lives of its citizens. A construal of government that reaches back as far as Aristotle has citizens defining the purpose or *telos* of the *polis* or state and supporting its philosophers in the formation of the requisite virtues within the populace. This construal—which enjoyed a renaissance in the birth of the American republic founded upon the pillars of Jerusalem and Athens—capitulated, under the influence of the liberal political theory growing out of the Enlightenment and traceable to Hobbes and Locke and refined in turn by Kant, Mill and finally John Rawls. The result was the less communal vision of government as the guarantor of individual rights and arbitrator in the disputes that inevitably arise when citizens lay claim to entitlements predicated on conflicting warrants.

What we have inherited, according to Sandel, are societies and governments no longer devoting their best talents and energy to a common vision of the good society and a robust (and inevitably often messy) public discussion regarding the virtues requisite to achieving it, but to the administration of a court system structured to adjudicate between citizens contending over alleged infringement of their personal rights.

---

2. Niebuhr, "The Idea of Covenant and American Democracy," 134.

3. Sandel, *Democracy's Discontent*.

In place of a communal dedication to the common good, the cultivation of public virtues capable of fostering that good, and the healthy balancing of rights and duties, we have embraced an individualistic worldview lacking meaningful social connections. Any remaining sediment of restraint on aggression and the unbridled accumulation of wealth and power comes to reside negatively in the fear of punishment under the law rather than in communal solidarity and mutual concern. The specter arises of devolution into a Machiavellian society resembling a jungle with everyone fighting for personal advantage and the prophetic voice appealing for dedication to common goals being drowned out by the clamor of citizen battling citizen.

In democratic societies with the threefold division of government inherited from traditional republicanism, that is, the Administrative, the Legislative, and the Judicial, the intended checks and balances become jeopardized by the waxing assertiveness of the Judiciary. The lofty vision of a republic caring for the needs of all citizens yields to a procedural democracy specializing in the pettifoggery of legal bureaucracy.

Far from rendering Niebuhr's thought obsolete, the enrichment of the debate over democracy by scholars like Robert Bellah, Michael Sandel, and more recently, Jeffrey Stout, only adds to the poignancy of his emphasis on covenant as a concept that we have left behind at great cost to the quality of our shared life. It therefore seems apropos to revisit Niebuhr's notion of covenant as the exercise of freedom that appears when citizens take "upon themselves the obligations of unlimited loyalty, under God, to principles of truthtelling, of justice, of loyalty to one another, of indissoluble union."[4]

In this definition, we find a standard against which the health of a democratic society can be measured. Especially in countries whose founding documents and subsequent development were shaped by a lively interplay between the traditions of Jerusalem and Athens, it seems reasonable to hope that fair-minded thinkers, regardless of political party affiliation or religious adherence, could agree that if governors and legislators and judges professed and practiced the moral qualities embedded in Niebuhr's definition, a

4. Niebuhr, "Idea of Covenant and American Democracy," 134.

foundation could be reconstructed for a just and compassionate society in which all citizens were encouraged to look beyond acquisitiveness and self-assertion to the higher goal of a society of shared dignity and well-being.

We shall move to examine the four moral principles that in Niebuhr's thought constitute the notion of covenant by relating them to recent developments in the country with which I am most familiar, the United States of America.

TRUTH-TELLING

"Truth-telling" has emerged in the media as well as in the halls of congress as a most earnest matter. Would U. S. engagement in Iraq with its consequent staggering monetary, and infinitely more tragic human costs have taken a different shape were it not for the repression and distortion of strategic information during the time in which a case was made for a massive military offensive? There is widespread agreement that the regime of Saddam Hussein was guilty of horrendous crimes against humanity. However, and as expressed already by George H. W. Bush in the first Iraq War (Desert Storm), the question of how to deal with Hussein was very complicated, both from a political and a military point of view.[5] While no simple solution was ever apparent, this much seems clear: The crisis called for leadership that was diligent in its gathering of accurate information and co-operative in working truthfully with other countries within the framework of the United Nations. Sadly, neither of these desiderata was followed. In one abrupt move, the U.S. withdrew from the U.N. debate and built a case for war on the basis of intelligence information that has proven to be grossly inaccurate, as well as on the repression of other sources that failed the test of confirming a military strategy that was already adopted.

In the meantime, truth-telling was under attack on the home front. A nation was facing a banking crisis that experts were comparing to the Great Depression. What would have been the state of the current housing and mortgage markets if simple truth-in-

5. Cf. Bush and Scowcroft, *World Transformed*, ch. 19

lending principles had been applied during the past decade of "easy money"? Countrywide, Bank of America, CitiCorp are names colored not only by news headlines but by personal experiences with unpredictably changing interest rates and deaf ears on the other end of the phone to the appeals of someone having been served a foreclosure notice.

Shifting attention to other segments of the business sector, the names Enron, Royal Dutch Shell, Tyco, and Halliburton have become infamous throughout the world for their accounting malpractices, coalition building with corrupt political regimes at the cost of peasant populations, unbridled greed on behalf of corporate leadership, and blatant profiteering. Halliburton, a huge, diversified oil exploration and supply company, serves as an example: While serving as the 46th Vice President of the United States, Dick Cheney, former CEO of Halliburton, apparently was untroubled by the aggressive lobbying of Halliburton representatives in Washington that led to lucrative contracts with the Pentagon--often in non-competitive bidding and with profit margins unjustifiable even under the conditions of war—for everything from mess-hall food to engine fuel in Iraq.[6] Though the silencing of whistle-blowers in Washington could have been offset by a stronger involvement of agencies like the UN, the then Secretary General's attention was being diverted by allegations of a family member misappropriating funds from the "Food for Oil" program. Blatantly clear in this example is the pernicious way in which lying spins an ever-widening web of corruption and oppression, a web threatening not only the industrial leaders of the past era, but emerging economies like India and China as well. And when it becomes apparent to common citizens that politicians, business leaders, and heads of world agencies share the same shady practices, it is virtually inevitable that the result will be cynicism and distrust. It is not long before the moment is reached that was lamented by the ancient Hebrew prophet: "truth stumbles in the public square" (Isaiah 59:14b).

---

6. Bad corporate habits prove tenacious. In the wake of the devastation caused by Hurricanes Katrina and Rita, lucrative contracts were once again garnered by the ever-nimble, globetrotting Halliburton.

JUSTICE

In the United States a center-stage promise in the 2004 presidential campaign was tax relief. Tax structure is a complicated economic issue, and the case can be made that the proper kind of tax reduction can invigorate the economy and thus produce jobs. To be just, however, such a strategy must include provisions for improving the quality of education for all children, for widening access to quality health care, and for job training. The growing gap in the first half of the twenty-first century between the very rich and the very poor indicates that current tax relief strategy is proving to be a faulty tool in the struggle for justice, since it is guided by priorities lacking in equal concern for all citizens.

An equally disturbing picture comes out of the history of our penal system. This can be illustrated by the debate revolving around capital punishment, encumbered by the irony that many of those advocating the rights of the unborn display few compunctions in executing convicted criminals, even in the wake of increasing evidence (especially that based on DNA testing) that executions have often been based on dubious evidence. Add to this the fact that the inmates lined up on death row consist overwhelmingly of those belonging to the economically marginalized and racially underrepresented, groups that have access to scant resources for self-defense. Should it not be disturbing to those adhering to the moral principle of impartial justice that access to essential human needs (rights!) like nutrition, health care, education, and fair trial often is determined by class and race?

The pernicious manner in which lying and injustice intertwine is displayed when one identifies the principal reason why a country as rich as the United States is falling far behind other industrial nations in contributing to the alleviation of world hunger and in redressing inequality in the provision of health service, education, and welfare to its own citizens: Its prioritizing of war over all other needs has resulted in the slashing of departmental budgets, with the notable exception of the Department of Defense. Martin Luther King's words continue to haunt us: "A nation that continues year after year to spend more money on military defense than on programs of social uplift is approaching spiritual death." Isaiah agrees: "Justice is turned back" (Isaiah 59:14).

LOYALTY TO ONE ANOTHER

Americans can be loyal, but all too often that loyalty is expressed within a tightly defined circle. Certainly the unilateral assertiveness that characterizes U.S. foreign policy has erected huge barriers between U.S. citizens and people throughout the world. But it is not only abroad that we are perceived to be a people withdrawn unto ourselves: More money is spent in our cities on personal security than on public police. The rich protect their wealth by living behind walls in gated communities. The human need for fellowship is fulfilled not within culturally and racially diverse communities, but within "lifestyle enclaves" or "affinity groups."[7] Even churches are affected, the membership of many of them resembling country clubs. Too often we seek comfort among people whose pigmentation is the same as ours, whose income level is similar, and even whose political views are compatible. Loyalty to one another in the rich sense intended by Niebuhr is in serious jeopardy.

INDISSOLUBLE UNION

The implosion of "one nation, indivisible" has been chronicled by author James Davison Hunter in his book *Culture Wars*.[8] Politicians prefer to blame the fractures in our countries on terrorists, anarchists, and illegal immigrants rather than acknowledging the egregious effects of abuse of public office for personal benefit, whether of a sexual or financial nature. Equally tragic is the breakdown of the otherwise very promising Middle East peace initiative by the Clinton administration amidst the Lewinski scandal and the foundering of the Bush Iraq policy under a barrage of allegations of profiteer-

7. Groundbreaking in the analysis of the retreat from traditional community prevalent in America are the studies of Robert N. Bellah, et al., *Habits of the Heart*; and *The Good Society*.

8. Hunter, *Culture Wars*.

ing and corruption. You cannot have indissoluble union when you have a betrayal of trust in the highest circles of governance. Rather than unifying their people around the noble causes of alleviating hunger, providing quality education and health care to all citizens, and being an example of generosity and peace-abiding humaneness throughout the world, the halls of leadership in the U.S. and many other countries abound with examples of the exploitation of power for personal gratification or benefit, mean-spirited partisanship, and fraud. Remarkable courage is required to speak out in a non-partisan manner on behalf of those who have slipped through the tattered safety nets of our societies into the anonymity and power-lessness of poverty and despair, or to jeopardize a promising future by exposing malfeasance or abuse of power in the workplace.

If Niebuhr is correct about the importance of covenant for the viability of a democratic republic, and if our evaluation is ac-curate, we have to ask what can be done to arrest the devolution into sharply divided and contentious societies. A common answer that one hears in our churches, synagogues, and mosques is this: Corruption in politics is not the responsibility of communities of faith, whose spiritual calling must not be distracted by shenanigans in Manila, Dehli, London or Washington. It is the responsibility of governing bodies and courts to clean up their own act. At best, faith communities can influence this process indirectly by providing spiritual sustenance for individuals who will go to fight for justice in their secular professions.

So much of what our ancestors sacrificed to achieve—justice, liberty, and equal opportunity—is threatened by the combination of brazen abuse of power and citizen apathy that the time has come when people of conscience must declare that the sharp partition-ing of faith and politics involves an impoverished understanding of both religion and public life. Theologically, it represents a betrayal of the central biblical teaching that God created one integrated uni-verse and declared it good and placed humans within it as stewards responsible for its preservation and flourishing and for tender-hearted care of one another.

Deeply grounded in Christian theology is the belief that included in God's plan for humanity is the provision of just and even-handed governance. As is evident in the narrative of both Testaments, God attends with special care for the poor and weak. It is the responsibility of government to maintain structures that ensure that wealth will be distributed fairly, courts will be impartial, and access to quality health care and education will be open to all. It should be evident that if public servants possess the moral qualities Niebuhr associates with covenant, equitable government will result.

It must also be recognized that Christian theology, especially in the Augustinian tradition, draws attention to "original sin," the human tendency to pervert good government and poison the quality of social life by the kinds of abuses we described earlier. Niebuhr was acutely aware of this tendency, and that awareness added a degree of urgency to the powerful qualification infused by the prepositional phrase "under God," inasmuch as it underlines the fact that the human being limited to its natural abilities is incapable of maintaining a just and equitable government and a humane and caring society and world.

Within Christianity, anthropology, broadly construed as the study of the essential qualities of human nature, has embodied the tension between depravity and promise, with the fulcrum located in the "under God" of Niebuhr's definition. This point is given specific confessional shape by Karl Barth's location of anthropology within Christology. It is the fallen condition of the human that is addressed by Christ, through whom the human is enabled to fulfill the destiny intended in creation for humanity and the cosmos. The Hebrew prophets, especially after the loss of temple and homeland to the Babylonians in 586 BCE, vividly portrayed the depravity and dignity of the human. Jeremiah despaired, "The human heart is devious above all else, it is perverse, who can understand it?" (Jeremiah 17:9). Only God was able, he concluded, and he looked to the time when a repentant people would experience re-birth through God's writing his commandments on the heart (Jeremiah 31:31–34). Ezekiel, similarly, professed that only God's re-creative act of replacing Israel's stone heart with a heart of flesh could result in a nation living in righteousness and security (Ezekiel 36:22–32). The Apostle Paul gave unforgettable expression to humanity's utter dependence on divine grace: "For I know that nothing good dwells in me, that is, in my flesh. I can will what is right, but I cannot do it" (Rom 7:18). It is hard to deny that lying at the heart of the Bible is a picture of unaided, unredeemed humanity as a hopeless creature.

Such Christian realism must be the starting point of a biblically based political theology, inasmuch as it testifies against excessive optimism based on a strictly humanistic construal of politics and issues a warning concerning illusions that mortals by nature will practice unlimited loyalty. However heroic the effort of human agents to create the good society, the good government, or even the good church, self-interest inevitably derails the project, unless the center of selfhood is shifted from the fearful, deceitful heart to the new creation that is a gift of God and to the indwelling of God's Spirit that transforms the will and draws it toward an all-inclusive goal transcending every human definition of the good. It is because of the Christian belief that such transformation transpires in the individual and the community through acceptance of God's gift in Christ that we believe that an authentic understanding of anthropology depends on a clear Christology and that a solid political philosophy depends on a profound theological understanding. Since this confessional position is not one that will be shared by vast numbers of the participants in the discourse of a diverse society, it will not be advanced *expressis verbis* as part of the negotiating strategy of the church. It will, however, provide an essential dimension of the perspective from which Christians view social and political issues and inform the moral positions they take in public debate. And as examples from history, ancient and modern, indicate, open debate conscientiously undertaken can lead to broad coalitions inclusive of many different religions and philosophies.

Let us sum up the central argument that we have made thus far: Due to the universal condition of the human being, individuals, by nature, are incapable of unlimited loyalty to the covenantal principles that are prerequisites for a healthy society, namely, truthtelling, justice, loyalty to one another, and indissoluble union. That is why a clear-headed Christian realist like Richard Niebuhr reintroduced into political reflection the traditional concept of covenant and resisted the modern tendency of reducing theological concepts to secular categories by insisting that covenant-making must occur "under God." Given the dismal record of modern democracies to achieve the high ideals written into their founding documents, we suggest that it is time for devout citizens to revisit the question of what it means to engage politics under God, and to do so in expectant discourse with fellow citizens, including those who do not share explicitly in traditional "god-talk."

This brings us to an important question: What does "under God" mean when related to the interaction of humans in society? We want to suggest that it revolves around acknowledgment of a transcendent Authority that relativizes all other authorities and powers. Further, it means surrendering to that Authority with a prayer that we will be freed from every form of earthly bondage, including those of our own making. And for Christians, it means accepting in repentance and gratitude the incalculable love and sacrifice of Christ and the new Creation of which we become a part when Christ becomes the center of our lives. It means recognizing that every personal need that led us to acts of greed and self-aggrandizement has been filled by the divine blessing flowing into the lives of the faithful, thereby creating in us the freedom to devote ourselves to that which transcends our personal desires, namely, an equitable society and a peaceful world. It means solidarity with all of those who have made God's purpose their purpose and thereby accepted as their vision for the world the one true government, the reign of God to which the prophets bore witness and the disciples experienced in following Jesus. In viewing the church as a partner God has chosen to continue the restoration of creation begun in Christ, the faithful are committed to discerning the ways in which the Gospel can guide their political activity within increasingly diverse and complex modern societies.

The challenge is demanding. To begin with, surrender to God and the transformation from natural self to new creation is anything but a casual affair, as is illustrated by the personal struggles that marked the lives of saints and martyrs from Jeremiah and the Apostle Paul to Dietrich Bonhoeffer, Oscar Romero, and Mother Teresa. And beyond the personal challenges entailed in living consistently as a disciple of Christ lies the daunting task of translating the moral principles of faith into the language and practices of politics in societies that are both multi-religious and largely secular. The common practice of consulting the Bible for an answer to a pressing domestic or international crisis and coming back with a verse contorted into yielding an unequivocal answer has left a trail of abuse that in the minds of many modern critics discredits the very notion of a theologically informed politics. In recognizing the impossibility of entering into a meaningful exploration of the whole range of issues entailed in a faithful political theology, we limit our task here to one preliminary question, "Where does the person of faith begin reflection on and practice of a biblically informed politics?"

We shall enter into this question by considering the example of the prophet Isaiah, asking what he had to say concerning truth-telling, justice, loyalty, and indissoluble union in his own society, and pondering whether his words sharpen issues facing people of faith in the modern world.

Truth-telling: "Woe you who call evil good, and good evil, who put darkness for light and light for darkness, who put bitter for sweet and sweet for bitter" (Isaiah 5:20).

Justice: "Woe to you who make inequitable decrees, who write oppressive laws, to turn aside the needy from justice, and to rob the poor people of their right, that widows may become your spoil, and that you may make orphans your prey. What will you do on the day of judgment? To whom will you flee for help? And where will you leave your wealth?" (Isaiah 10:1).

Loyalty to one another: "The Lord enters into judgment with the elders and princes of his people. It is you who have devoured the vineyard, the spoil of the poor is in your houses. What do you mean by crushing my people, by grinding the face of the poor in the dust?" says the Lord God of Hosts (Isaiah 3:15).

Indissoluble union: "The people will oppress one another, everyone his fellow and everyone his neighbor; the youth will be insolent to the elder, and the base fellow to the honorable" (Isaiah 3:5).

Our first response to these words may be one of despair and resignation: For 2,700 years, nothing has changed, the same exploitation of the poor through the corrupt practices of the powerful, the same denial of the rights of the weak through perversion of the law, the same accumulation of wealth by the few to the impoverishment of the many. In the U.S., the cry arises from increasing throngs of urban and rural poor, day laborers, new immigrants, single mothers, impoverished retirees and the infirm as they hear election campaign promises of relief, but witness decidedly less commitment to quality-of-life issues like education and health and financial capability of retaining ownership of their homes than to military appropriations, corporate bailouts and reduction of taxes on capital gains. Even when election results, such as those in the 2008 presidential campaign, indicate that the voices of many of those who have been left out of the political process are being heard and are influencing the shape of public policies and appointments, cynicism remains widespread: "Will genuine change occur, can special-privilege politics be dislodged, can corruption be overcome, can richly funded lobbying on the part of powerful corporations be counterbalanced by moral discrimination?" While cynicism is hardly to be commended at a time when positive changes in areas like health care, tax reform, and suitable government regulation seem possible, the temptation to abandon watchfulness and prophetic witness must be resisted on the basis of a clear recognition of the limitations endemic to every human institution given the ubiquity of partisan rivalry and vested self-interest.

We opened our discussion in the first chapter by noting that not only economically but in terms of the human family, the world has become a global community. Therefore, it should come as no surprise that the temptations of both cynicism and sloth are widespread in most modern nations. In the Philippines, for example, in the face of spreading joblessness, poverty, and crime, campaign promises for the betterment of the lives of the poor are met with reactions ranging from violence to resignation. As one thoughtful Manila merchant explained to me, "First we had EDSA 1 followed by corruption and poverty, then we had EDSA 2, followed by more corruption and poverty, and now we have EDSA 3 . . ."[9] When the

9. EDSA is the acronym for the main highway the encircles Manila (Epifanio de los Santos Avenue). It was the scene of demonstrations that led

seemingly inexorable decline in the quality of life of the majority of humans is viewed on a worldwide scale, it becomes apparent why radical religio-political movements bringing food and healthcare and education—unfortunately, often in the company of those who promote terrorist tactics—are finding fertile recruiting ground in Iraq, Pakistan, Afghanistan, Malasia, Sri Lanka, and the southern islands of the Philippines.

In many parts of the world, it seems justified that the victims of neglect and oppression blame their ills on "those in power." And so it was in antiquity: Jews suffering under Antiochus IV were justified in that response, for they were an oppressed minority lacking political influence. The same was true of Christians suffering under Nero and Diocletian. And Christians, Jews, and other religious communities living in many parts of the world today, including India, Tibet, Egypt, Iraq and Iran, have little influence on the authorities that govern their daily lives. But what excuse can be made for Christians living in nations with strong roots in Christian tradition and with church members occupying positions of authority in all branches of government? We *have* no excuse! We must accept responsibility for rampant lying, injustice, corruption, and the abuse of power. But how do we move from confessions of complacency to effective strategies of reform?

It is fashionable for Christians to join the ranks of "the experts" by adopting the language and strategies of the political sciences and offering answers in the form of economic theories, schemes driven by social engineering, and foreign policy making. This is often the role assumed by Christians and Jewish advisors once they become a part of the Washington establishment. This is not to dismiss the importance of expert economic or political advice provided by experts in such fields who happen to be Christians or Jews. But being a Christian or a Jew or a Muslim or a Buddhist does not create expertise in the diverse and complicated departments of human knowledge or provide a scientific "edge" over a non-believing col-

---

to the overthrow of the Ferdinand Marcos government in 1986 (EDSA 1), the Joseph Estrada administration in 2001 (EDSA 2), and has continued to be the gathering point of demonstrations against the Gloria Macapagal-Arroyo regime (EDSA 3).

league. Luther's children had better sandals because he preferred a
Turkish shoemaker who was good at his trade over a Christian who
was mediocre. But the most important reason Christians should not
be deluded into thinking that faith automatically creates scientific
knowledge is that such illusions impede recognition of the area
in which faith does foster discernment, namely, understanding of
the human heart (deceitful yet not beyond the reach of divine forgiveness and grace), and understanding of the nature of the union
sought by the redeemed heart with a cause that transcends every
human desire and encompasses all creation.

Certainly Isaiah, in looking at a seemingly incorrigible people,
was tempted to despair. But he directed his energy toward a more
constructive goal and, in so doing, was guided by the concept of
covenant. Like Niebuhr, he understood his nation's crisis as more
than a neglect of the moral principles of truth, justice, and loyalty.
On the deepest level, he perceived that Israel had abandoned her
commitment to that which holds a moral universe together, namely,
the "under God" of the covenant relationship (Isaiah 1:2–3). He over-
heard this twisted reasoning: "We have made a covenant with death!
And with Sheol we have made an agreement, for we have made lies
our refuge and in falsehood we have taken shelter." Ancient Israel's
leaders were not without a covenant to structure their affairs, but it
was not a covenant certified by God. Accordingly, it led not to life
but to death; in the case of the Northern Kingdom, to death under
the ruthless might of Assyria; in the case of Judah, during Jeremiah's
time, to death under the armies of the Babylonians.

We grasp less than the full picture, however, if we fail to see
that the leaders of Israel and Judah did not share the assessment of
the prophets. To them, their policies, based on international diplo-
macy and confidence in military might, provided a secure basis for
national security. Prophetic criticism that called into question their
strategies was condemned as treason. Heads of state and their advisors argued that, especially during a time of national crisis, every
patriot would stand behind the central government and the military
establishment supporting official policies. Jeremiah, in declaring
that Judah's relationship with God did not guarantee her immunity
to destruction by a foreign power, encountered the condemnation

of the king's advisors: "This man ought to be put to death, because he is discouraging the soldiers who are left in this city, and all the people, by speaking such words to them. For this man is not seeking the welfare of this people, but their harm" (Jeremiah 38:4). History, of course, proved that the true patriot was the one who dared to name the perverted covenant for what it was, a covenant with death based on nationalistic idolatry. But that did not end application of the political stratagem of silencing criticism by labeling it treason.

In our time as in the time of Israel's prophets, one of the most lethal policies is the one that identifies faith with blind patriotism. History has demonstrated time and again that nations rise and fall, and God's reign is identified with no earthly entity. Moreover, the most potent agent in hastening the decline of any empire is the hubris of exceptionalism, of special privilege, of the illusion of manifest destiny claiming divine authorization for the unilateral determination of the destiny of other peoples. Such pride rests securely on the self-designation of the new humanity as the center of the universe, in need of no god but its own limitless potential. Such is the nature of the covenant of death bequeathed by misapplication of the insights of the Enlightenment.

Taking the example of Isaiah, should we not make despair our refuge? Not if we read on, for the blustering words of confidence by Israel's leaders in their self-fashioned covenant was not the last word. God replied:

> See, I am laying in Zion a foundation stone,
>   a tested stone,
> a precious cornerstone, a sure foundation:
>   "One who trusts will not panic."
> And I will make justice the line,
>   and righteousness the plummet;
> hail will sweep away the refuge of lies,
>   and waters will overwhelm the shelter.
> Then your covenant with death will be annulled,
>   and your agreement with Sheol will not stand."
> (Isaiah 28:16–18)

Isaiah was delivered from despair by having his focus directed solely on the reign that survives the passing of empires, an eternal, universal reign built upon righteousness. Isaiah was summoned to trust in the reality of that government, and to continue in his testimony that only to the extent that earthly governments build upon that tested stone would they experience any degree of security and health.

Trust in the only reality that can provide the foundation for a nation's health, courage to declare every other purported basis for national security a seductive trap, and discernment to offer dependable advice to national leaders regarding domestic and foreign crises; where did Isaiah find the source of such rare qualities? Did he turn to the sages? To the philosophical academies? To the temple scribes? There is every reason to believe that Isaiah was trained in the most advanced knowledge that all of the above had to provide. But by his own testimony in Isaiah 6, we learn that his fundamental source was located not in academic institutions, but in worship. The touchstone of all of his political action was found in the presence of the Holy One of Israel. There he exposed his heart to the only true Ruler, the Ruler of all nations, the Creator of the universe, and emptied of pride and self-assertion, he confessed: "Woe is me for I am a man of unclean lips, and I dwell among a people of unclean lips, mine eyes have seen the king, the Lord of hosts" (Isaiah 6:5). This is not to suggest that Isaiah's experience of God's presence was purely emotional or subjective, for his words and actions bespeak thorough knowledge of his religious tradition combined with detailed acquaintance with the concrete economic and political realities of his nation and the international conflicts that had engulfed the Eastern Mediterranean during his lifetime. But the sum total of such expertise does not provide the key to his powerful message to the Jewish nation and its leaders. The key that energized his witness was the personal experience that history was not the product of human design, neither was it the result of pure accident; history was the arena of divine purpose. Hence the witness of one who was granted insight into that purpose was of critical importance for a nation charting its course through the precarious waters of domestic crises and international conflicts. For Isaiah, the starting point of his political engagement was the numinous moment of finding himself in the presence of the Sovereign One, the radical reorienting moment of worship.

From that numinous experience, a chastened Isaiah ventured forth under God's command, "Go and tell my people . . ." (Isaiah 6:9). In worship, Isaiah had come to the realization that God alone could unveil the lies, distortions, and injustices of his nation. Before the holiness of God, the corruption and presumptuousness of the world's leaders came to light. And only there, in the presence of the Holy One, did the gravity of Israel's crisis come to light (Isaiah 6:9–13).

From Isaiah's example, we draw an audacious conclusion: For Christian political action to maintain a dependable, truthful foundation, it must be grounded in worship. In worship, the person and community of faith recognize that there is only one Ruler who can make an absolute claim on one's conscience. The other institutions of which we are a part, including nation-state and church, are important aspects of our life together, but they can exercise at most a penultimate authority, that is, an authority that is binding only to the extent that it conforms to and promotes the justice, harmony, and humaneness that are intrinsic to God's universal rule. On this basis, the church dares to claim that worship is the most important political action in which it engages!

The indispensable role of worship in the political engagement of people of faith may not be very evident during times of relative normalcy. The situation is vastly different when a country is overwhelmed by a totalitarian regime insisting on the absolute loyalty of its subjects. In the case of the Soviet Union, this led to attempts to silence the church through indoctrination in an atheistic worldview where state became the Absolute. In the case of Nazi Germany, the attempt was made to identify church teaching with the ideology of state, and in the 1930s, that attempt enjoyed widespread support among leaders of the German Church. They bestowed the honors of state on theologians who distorted Romans 13 and Luther's two kingdoms teaching into a strict separation of church and state, with the influence of the church being limited strictly to the realm of the spirit, while the state, with the blessing of the church, was to enjoy absolute authority over all matters pertaining to social and economic order and national security.

The National Socialist response to the Christian resistance (the "Confessing Church") took the form of ruthless suppression. Asserting the absolute authority inherent in fascist ideology, it could not tolerate the prophetic testimony that no earthly government possessed authority over the conscience of its citizens. Hans Lilje, Dietrich Bonhoeffer, Rudolf Bultmann, and their fellow confessors were declared traitors to the Fatherland for daring to condemn the measures being taken to rid Germany of Jews, Gypsies, the mentally disabled, and other groups deviating from the Arian paradigm. In reading the literature of the Confessing Church during its years of underground activity and persistent persecution, one theme arises more emphatically than any other: it was a worshipping community. In its most critical moments of political decision, such as the decision to attempt to assassinate Adolf Hitler, Bonhoeffer and his associates deliberated amidst unceasing worship and prayer with the firm conviction that their consciences were bound by one Authority alone, and that their only hope, in this world and in the world to come, was found in the shadow of the Almighty.

To establish the primacy of worship in the life of faith is not yet to complete the picture of a life modeled after the prophets and Jesus Christ. Especially in periods of social unrest and duress, worship can be construed as a haven from the storm. Worship can lead to an escape from the political fray as one awaits God's intervention either to raise the faithful to a realm unsullied by injustice or to impose God's reign by force. The covenanters of ancient Qumran withdrew to the shores of the Dead Sea to await that intervention. The apocalyptic writer of 4 Ezra heard God command him keep from the public the esoteric writings that had been placed in his safekeeping. In contrast to the closed-conventicle posture of apocalyptic seers, the prophet Isaiah—like all true prophets before and after him—was commanded to proclaim publicly the prescient words and proceedings he had witnessed, "Go and say to my people . . ." Prophetic worship as practiced by Isaiah is not self-indulgent: Beginning in the depths of his being, it moves outward to embrace the wider world. As seductive as it may be to remain enraptured by the incense, hymnody, and drama of the heavenly throne room, and as theologically correct as it may be to describe the ultimate human vocation as that of glorifying God with the angelic hosts in eternity, the near-term mandate of worship is to relate God's word to human existence. In contemporary parlance, that means "getting political."

The same prophetic lesson is taught by the New Testament story of the Transfiguration. James, Peter, and John witnessed Jesus speaking with Moses and Elijah. Peter said: "Lord, it is good for us to be here; if you wish, I will make three dwellings here, one for you, one for Moses, and one for Elijah" (Matthew 17:4). The disciples were granted a brilliant moment of epiphany and worship, but the temptation to make the beatific arrangement permanent was rebuffed. As suddenly as their moment of heavenly vision came, it disappeared, and they found themselves in the company of Jesus alone, and as was his wont, he led them right back into a world of human need and widespread suffering inflicted by both Roman and demonic legions.

The world of human need and suffering is where worship, in the company of the Lord, has led disciples throughout the centuries. To ignore the commissioning is to miss a dimension intrinsic to worship. But to enter the fray without acknowledging the starting point in worship is to engage the messy world of politics without adequate grounding and orientation. Worship and world are inseparable components of the life of faith.

It is inevitable that the worship–world dialectic that shapes the life of faith will entail trial and testing. Isaiah left the Holy One's presence only to encounter a people seemingly incapable of hearing God's word. Jesus led James, Peter, and John from their transfiguring experience into the midst of "a faithless and perverse generation" (Matthew 17:17). The latter story gives a fuller picture of discipleship than the former by describing how the disciples did not leave their worship experience unaccompanied, but in the presence of their Lord. And indeed, the narrative continues, beyond their Lord's eventual departure, to describe how they were not abandoned by God even then, but placed under the protection of the Holy Spirit. When acknowledging worship as the "touchstone" of Christian political action, therefore, we must never forget that worship is not a launching pad, from which we are catapulted singlehandedly into a struggle, but the space providing renewal of the relationship in the company of God's Spirit. The task to which we are sent is nothing less than to share the New Creation of which we have become a part with the entire world through acts of kindness, advocacy, and peacemaking. Paul uses an apt metaphor for this task, "So we are ambassadors for Christ, since God is making his appeal through us ..." (2 Corinthians 5:20).

In Romans 8, Paul applies this dialectic to his personal life when he explains his own sufferings as part of a cosmic drama, in which God has subjected creation "to futility . . . in hope." Seeing life's struggles from the perspective of God's plan does not banish pain and struggle, but diminishes their significance, given the incomparability of the renewal of creation of which God's ambassadors become a part. And like the Gospel narrative, so too Paul ends his musing with a hymn celebrating the utter impotency of every evil power to separate the faithful "from the love of God in Christ Jesus our Lord" (Romans 8:38–39).

If the Church hopes to clarify its relation to the political realm, it must return to the lessons of Scripture. Careful study of both Testaments makes it abundantly clear that political parties and secular movements, when they are dedicated to justice and equality and do not claim absolute conscience-binding authority, have a place in a biblical understanding of world order (e.g., Romans 13:1–7). But in that order, the church is called not to replicate the efforts of such parties and movements, but to accept the role of representing the only universal government that relativizes all human institutions and provides the norms that define their mandate and against which they are to be evaluated and judged. We can catch this lesson by paraphrasing the Apostle Paul, "we regard no political party, no national government, from a human point of view" (2 Corinthians 5:16). What people of faith bring to politics is a freedom to advise, criticize, and strategize based on an ultimate allegiance that is reserved for God alone.

The transcendent perspective brought by the person of faith to politics has the potential to enrich political discourse and, ultimately, to contribute to the health of society and its branches of government. It is a perspective that identifies corruption, cronyism, and defective policy not merely as mismanagement, but as reflections of defects rooted in the human heart and reachable only by conversion and spiritual renewal. Within our communities of faith, the challenge is to make more vivid the call to conversion from the habits of this world and to present the excitement and joy of becoming active participants in God's renewal and healing of humanity and world. In the public realm, where one must be aware of the presence of participants from other faiths or no faith and, hence, must seek to translate specifically Christian confessions into terms comprehensible to others, the transcendent perspective of faith can nevertheless provide a depth dimension to the assessment of issues and crises, even as it can contribute a wealth of wisdom, a dependable source of courage, and a basis for humility and self-critique. It is because this unique perspective becomes available to humans by divine grace that we state yet again the audacious claim that, for Christians, the authentic starting point for political action is worship.

It is necessary, albeit briefly, to consider the challenge faced in seeking to share the specific Christian vision of the human condition and God's redemptive purpose with the wider society. When we move from worship into the world, we not only face human injustice, sickness, hunger, and international conflict, we encounter fellow humans, potential allies in the renewal and healing of the world, who do not share our religion.

It is not possible to delineate one strategy, since the religious landscape differs widely from one country to the next. In most of Europe, Christians must be prepared to speak to a largely secular public. In the U.S. parts of South America, many countries of Africa, Korea and the Philippines, biblical faith is still widely shared within the population. To be sure, differences between these countries is very great. Let us, as an example of similarities and differences, consider the United States and the Philippines.

In the United States, the politically most assertive form of Christianity comes from the Religious Right. In the 2004 presidential election, that coalition represented 18 percent of the Republican vote. Its approach to issues like abortion, gay marriage, and Middle Eastern policy tends to be more absolutist in nature than many mainline Christians feel comfortable with. When hermeneutical absolutism is wedded to an ideology of "manifest destiny"—that is, belief in a special role assigned to the U.S. in divine purpose—critics, both Christian and non-Christian, express their concern using terms like *Pax Americana* and nationalistic idolatry. Unfortunately, the exploitation of the Bible in defense of national self-interest and imperialist policies is evident at many points in U.S. history, including the first decade of the twentieth century when the case was being made in Congress for annexation of the Philippines. Yet, if one thing is clear in the biblical case we have made for worship as the touchstone of Christian political action, it is this: In addressing politics, the Christian must be aware that God favors no one nation over others, that God loves every member of the human family, wherever that person lives, and that God condemns as idolatry and a mockery of the living God the national hubris that exploits religion for personal and national self interest.

In the Philippines, we find a situation in which roughly 80 percent of the population is Roman Catholic. Here nearly all political leaders (with the exception of anarchists and some of the insurgents) present themselves as faithful in worship, and by implication under divine blessing. It is notable that the major political parties include celebration of the Mass in their conferences. A friend from Manila recently satirized the situation thus: God looks down from heaven and notices that political party X begins its conference with a priest celebrating the Mass, then God notices party Y doing the same, and so on, which leads to a bit of confusion in the divine assembly and debate over religious-political alliances. While on the surface the Philippine situation differs from the one in the U.S., the deeper question remains the same, "When does the wedding of religion with party politics lapse into idolatry?" Newspapers reported that in 2005 President Arroyo, under the weight of impeachment threats, prayed and placed her situation in God's care. Christians can rejoice over prayerful soul-searching on the part of their leaders, but at the same time the church must maintain its prophetic role of insisting that God is the unconditional guarantor and servant of no political regime. Priestly ministry of the church to political leaders must live in tension with the kind of prophetic witness illustrated by the lengthy public fast observed in Manila during the Philippine crisis of 2005 by a local Roman Catholic priest as a protest against political corruption and broken promises regarding the poor and unemployed.

While ambiguities will abound as we move from one country to another and one situation to another, we must remain clear that we will be best equipped to exercise our political responsibility as Christian individuals and communities if we remain firmly grounded in the Bible. We will become sensitive to the abuse of worship, for example, by the divine rebuke delivered by Isaiah to those misusing worship in his day: "When you come to appear before me, who asked this from your hand? Trample my courts no more . . . When you stretch out your hands, I will hide my eyes from you; even though you make many prayers, I will not listen; your hands are full of blood. Wash yourselves; make yourselves clean; remove the evil of your doings from before my eyes; cease to do evil, learn to do good; seek justice, rescue the oppressed, defend the orphan, plead for the widow" (Isaiah 1:12–17). We can also be placed on guard against worship that simply becomes a formality, "these people draw near with their mouths, and honor me with their lips, while their hearts are far from me, and their worship of me is a human commandment learned by rote" (Isaiah 29:13). Worship can become emptied of meaning when a hymn, a prayer, a liturgy is recited without awareness of the presence of the living God whose heart is filled with compassion for the hungry, the oppressed, the bereaved, the homeless and friendless.

The inextricable connection between worship and everyday living was central to Isaiah's thought. In true worship, the person of faith offers up to God all that one is, including the acts of kindness of the previous week, and in God's presence blessing and renewal are received in abundance. We dare not forget that worship is not just coming to get an uplifting experience on Sunday, it is advocating for marginalized families removed from homes lost through foreclosure, for the elderly and infirm living along rivers and train lines in squatter huts, for women languishing in overcrowded hospital compounds awaiting treatment for HIV/AIDS. Worship is to remind leaders of their ultimate moral responsibility to the citizens of all nations and to the threatened natural environment that is our fragile home. It is responding to cries for help from innocent men, women and children ravaged by political dereliction and violence in Darfur, Ruwanda and Zimbabwe. Worship is praying, "your kingdom come, your will be done, on earth as it is in heaven," and living that kingdom in everyday life.

The Apostle Paul offers a poignant lesson in true worship. The worshipping community is not just a group that hears in Scripture words of judgment on dishonest leaders and then declares its condemnation of its own elected officials. The church is a community that embodies within its internal life the justice, compassion and equality that it calls forth in others. It provides a model of the good society. In 1 Corinthians 11:17–22, Paul makes this very concrete by observing something scandalous in the church in Corinth. He notices that the people are celebrating the Eucharist and he describes their outrageous behavior: "for in eating each one goes ahead with his or her own meal. One is hungry and the other is drunk." Does that describe the situation in our churches? Are we aware that the Eucharist is not just a church social, that it is the celebration of the heavenly banquet including all of God's children, on earth as it is in heaven?

If the Eucharist is degraded into being a meal in our various churches in which the very divisions that tear at the fabric of the human family are reflected, if the Lord's supper abets the social stratification and economic inequality that dehumanizes our citizens, such that in one congregation the rich gather to feast, in another the poor huddle to commiserate, in one congregation the powerful reinforce useful business connections, in another the marginalized fluctuate between anger and resignation, then we fall under the judgment pronounced by Paul for those who replace the body of Christ with a farce by preparing a sumptuous feast for themselves in callous disregard for neighbors in need (1 Corinthians 11:27–29).

Perhaps the most hard-hitting warning against perverted worship was delivered in Jeremiah 7. The situation was dire. Judah and its capital city Jerusalem were about to be reduced to an ash heap by the Babylonian armies. But the people remained smugly confident. After all, the temple was ensconced in their city, God dwelt in their midst, and God was ready to defend them. Enter Jeremiah: "Do not trust in these words: the temple of the LORD, the temple of the LORD, the temple of the LORD ... Will you steal, murder, commit adultery, swear falsely ... and then come and stand in this house which is called by my name and say, 'We are safe!'—only to go on doing all these abominations?" (7:4, 9–10). On the cusp of national disaster, Jeremiah made a last-ditch attempt to bring the people back to a proper understanding of worship: "If you truly amend your ways and your doings, if you truly act justly one with another, if you do not oppress the alien, the orphan, and the widow, or shed innocent blood in this place, and if you do not go after other gods to our hurt, then I will dwell with you in this place, in the land that I gave of old to your ancestors forever and ever" (7:5–7).

Instructed by prophetic leaders of our own era and chastened by Scripture, we must continue to reflect on our vocation as Christians in our respective settings and renew our living commitments. Hopefully, we will understand that for us to address politics faithfully, we have to open ourselves to God in worship, be brought to an understanding of God's redemptive purpose for the world, and experience worship as the integrative, all-embracing center of our public and private lives. And we dare not forget the warning of Jeremiah that we are living in a crisis that demands urgent response, a crisis in which our twin assault on nature and the fabric of human community threatens life as we have taken it for granted for centuries. As we respond, H. Richard Niebuhr, by calling our attention to the collapse of the sense of covenant in our interactions with one another and its dire consequences, also invites us to the process of healing that can renew health and vitality in nation and world, a process that will restore among us truth-telling, justice, loyalty to one another, and indissoluble union, for these are the four points that constitute a reliable moral compass for any individual or community committed to genuine citizenship. While the coalition of committed citizens will include members of all faiths and worldviews, it is the special responsibility of those who are heirs to biblical faith to represent, as a dependable leaven, the undergirding and inspiriting dimension represented by the phrase, "under God."

We end with a text that brings into one intimate unity the God we worship, the vocations to which we are called, and the members of the all-inclusive family that Christ loved and served, Matthew

25:31–46. We are treated to high drama: The Son of Man is seated on his throne to judge the nations. Goats are separated out and sent to hell. The sheep, on the other hand, are invited to the eternal kingdom, for when the Son of Man was hungry, thirsty, lonely, naked, sick, and in prison, they went to care for him. Their response is unforgettable: "When did we thus care for you?" To which the mighty Judge responds, "as you did it to one of the least of these who are members of my family, you did it to me."

But what does this familiar story have to do with worship, Eucharist, the Mass? It points to the central point of Christian worship! It asks, Whom do we seek as we share bread and wine with one another? What do we encounter in those basic life-sustaining gifts and in the accompanying words that draw attention to the banquet's host? We are brought to the awareness that we are not simply eating bread and drinking wine, we are receiving the body and blood of our Lord! Matthew 25 provides us with an essential lesson about worship. We seek our Lord as the deepest passion of our lives, and Matthew 25 tells us where he is to be found, where it is that we encounter our Host and receive the invitation to be with Him forever. Great is the incarnation mystery, linking worship and the imprisoned, the Lord and the thirsty, the banquet in heaven and the homeless shelter in the church basement. We are all to be links in a chain that is rusty and golden, mundane and heavenly, a chain designed not to enslave but to release slaves, not to bind but to restore a debased earth and a fractured human family, with the result that the grain scattered over the face of the earth will be gathered into loaves of bread for all those who hunger. Such is the worship to which we are called, and if we accept the invitation, it will have everything to do with the way we engage in politics.

3 *Covenant and Politics*

In the previous two chapters we engaged in exploration of the challenges facing persons of faith who seek to balance faithfulness to scriptural and confessional heritage with sensitivity to the religious and philosophical diversity that characterizes their particular nation-state. We described that balance as one charged with a lively tension, with the specific communitarian experiences of worship and eschatological hope serving as bookends in a hermeneutical movement that also demands sensitivity to speak specific truths and convictions in a language comprehensible to fellow-citizens whose religious beliefs and moral principles are rooted in other scriptures and traditions. We found the theological and social-ethical thought of H. Richard Niebuhr particularly helpful as an example of how a central tenet of biblical faith can enrich public understanding of moral imperatives that are essential foundation stones for a society dedicated to equality and justice. Key to Niebuhr's analysis was the notion of "covenant," in which the qualities of truth-telling, justice, loyalty, and indissoluble union provide the cohesion prerequisite for the good society, qualities, moreover, that become anemic if separated from an authorizing warrant that transcends human agents. "Under God" was accordingly seen to provide a vital connection between confessional beliefs and moral principles in a society that is able to maintain the lively balance between religion and politics.

In this chapter we shall look more deeply into the concept of "covenant," for any argument defending its importance in public discourse must deal with the fact that its meaning and significance remain quite foreign to the thought of most people today. Aside from biblical scholars, does anyone use the word anymore in everyday speech? Deeming the question worthy at least of cursory investigation, I scanned several newspapers and weekly periodicals and listened to "The News Hour with Jim Lehrer." Negative results confirmed my suspicion. This led to a second phase of my "research," the file in my study marked "legal documents." My search was rewarded in discovering this sentence in the warranty deed for the purchase of our family home: "I do covenant with the said Grantees, their heirs and assigns, that I am lawfully seized in fee of the premises." The scope of my query thus was enlarged with this discovery of a second profession familiar with the language of covenant. But why is it that lawyers, alone alongside theologians, persist in using this rather archaic term? The answer seems patent: In drawing up quit claims and warranty deeds, lawyers cannot tolerate situations in which agreements are not upheld. Consequently, they use the strongest word available in the English language to urge truth-telling and the honoring of obligations—namely, *covenant*.

The rest of society in the meantime seems content to have discarded the term altogether. To "covenant with" someone would sound about as silly in colloquial discourse as for the young suitor to get down on one knee and announce to his loved one, "I plight thee mine troth." The essential question that arises from this brief excursion into contemporary idiom is this: Can we remain content to leave the language of covenant-making to lawyers and the few medieval lords and ladies remaining in our society, or should we be concerned that something has been lost in the political realm as a result of the abandonment of this once-revered concept? It should be of some concern to us that, as we observed in the last chapter, no less a sage of modern culture than H. Richard Niebuhr argued that the idea of covenant is crucial for the preservation of a democratic republic.[1] From a historical perspective, according to Niebuhr, covenant stands out as categorically different from related contractual concepts used by political theorists. For example, the hierarchical model prevalent in medieval thought failed to capture the dynamic of reciprocity that is present in covenant, according to which binding promises are made by both parties rather than solely by the vassal to the suzerain. In later Calvinist thought, a mechanistic understanding placed emphasis on the self-regulating nature of agreements between parties, an emphasis that carried over into

1. Niebuhr, "Idea of Covenant and American Democracy."

Deism in keeping with its diminution of the personal dimension in the divine/human relationship. Finally, the notion of contract that played a dominant role in much British political philosophy stressed the mutual benefits derived by the participating parties but added a hedging provision that compromised the binding nature of the commitments. One party could back out of the agreement, and to the degree that power arrangements between the contractual parties were unequal, the ease with which the more powerful could annul the contract was increased.

How does covenant differ from the above-mentioned constructs for formalizing an agreement between two parties? As we have seen, in a covenant the parties, as an exercise of free will, take upon themselves "the obligations of unlimited loyalty, under God, to principles of truth-telling, of justice, of loyalty to one another, of indissoluble union."[2] Any civil society will regard as essential to its viability the principles of truth-telling, justice, mutual loyalty, and indissoluble union. And indeed, a secular construal of political theory will stress the importance of these principles and urge conformity to the conditions they describe. But the theo-politics of Niebuhr presses further by asking where a reliable basis can be found for these principles. The answer given by Niebuhr is found in the juxtaposition of the terms "unlimited loyalty" and "under God." "Unlimited loyalty" is a quality of commitment that can be assumed no matter how circumstances change and independent of the immediate benefits or sacrifices that befall either side. Such loyalty derives its force from acknowledgment on the part of the human parties of a Guarantor transcending the arbitrariness and compromises of conventional power politics. What this contributes to a body politic is a moral grounding that derives its authority not merely from human promises but above all from an ultimate Reality upon whom all citizens are dependent. Since instances of "unlimited loyalty" are rare, one looks to something as extraordinary as the history of martyrs for illustration of its nature. For example, what was it that bound Dietrich Bonhoeffer to a moral obligation to remain steadfast in his opposition to the Nazis even when it mandated a course of action leading to execution? The last words of his poem

2. Ibid., 134.

"Who Am I?" give the answer: "Whoever I am, Thou knowest, O God, I am thine!"[3] Whatever other loyalties were woven into his existence—family, fiancée, nation, church—they were all subsumed under and integrated into his ultimate loyalty to God.

The notion of unconditional loyalty to God raises the question of fanaticism, especially during times when terrorist acts frequently are justified by religious zeal. The classic philosophical case against the justification of immoral acts by appeal to divine revelation was made by Immanuel Kant. His position that the categorical status of universal moral principles trumps appeal to the human *perception* of divine command represents one of the most urgent ethical challenges facing traditions that appeal to divine revelation for guidance in responding to contemporary issues.[4] It cannot be denied that religious fanaticism has perpetrated horrendous deeds from the medieval Crusades to the attack on the World Trade Center towers in 2001. How can such perversion of religion in the service of reckless and (judged from the perspective of widely held standards of human decency) immoral political stratagems be refuted within a worldview that calibrates its moral compass on the basis of a Reality transcending all things human, including human reason?

Again, we are instructed by the example of Dietrich Bonhoeffer. From a Kierkegaardian point of view, his participation in the attempt to stem the rising tide of genocide under the Nazis by assassinating Adolf Hitler could be ascribed to the concept of the "teleological suspension of ethical."[5] God had given his command, and faith, whether in the case of Abraham or a member of the Confessing Church, called for unquestioning submission to divine will. But Bonhoeffer's faith was categorically different from such "blind" faith. Indeed, no struggle commanded his attention more that that of reconciling faith and ethics, and that meant coming to grips with the temptation of being seduced into premature certainty by an over-facile reliance on faith understood as a construct rather the response to a living relationship with the God known in the suffering Christ.

3. Bonhoeffer, *Cost of Discipleship*, 15.

4. Kant, *Critique of Pure Reason*, 644 [A 818f, B 846f].

5. Kierkegaard, *Fear and Trembling and The Book on Adler*, 45–58.

So committed was he to wrestling with the ambiguities entailed in ethical reflection that it is reported that following Hitler's successful occupation of Paris he raised the dreadful question at a church conference of whether that event would have to be understood in terms of divine purpose! Clearly Bonhoeffer's Lutheran faith did not exclude the rigorous exercise of human ethical discernment, an exercise that required diligence and prayer within the context of fellow believers. His decision to participate in the plan to assassinate Hitler accordingly was shaped not in the brilliant certitude of a personal revelation, but in the caldron of communal worship and study within an underground Church that chose discipleship over patriotism and loyalty to the *Führer*.[6]

The lesson we are given from the position taken by Bonheoffer and his fellow confessors revolves around the ethical corollary of his belief that God was the author of the universal moral order binding on all humans. The case had to be demonstrated that an act that broke a universally held moral law (in this case the prohibition of murder) in fact was justified by a higher moral principle deriving from God's sovereignty. No individual held the license to make such a dread determination on his or her own authority. The implicit reasoning underlying this strategy can be formulated as follows for any religious community dedicated to the concept of universal justice and compassion: Any case for a human endeavor by appeal to religious warrants that contradicts moral norms held by the civilized communities of the world and centrally located in the religious and philosophical classics of those communities must be repudiated. But does this general principle allow for exceptions *in extremis*?

Søren Kierkegaard's concept of the "teleological suspension of the ethical," if perhaps formulating the challenge of extreme exceptions too starkly, nevertheless presses its fundamental underlying question: Is it justifiable, ethically or theologically, under any circumstance, to obey a divine word if it entails what would widely

---

6. Bonhoeffer was one of the leading members of the "Confessing Church" (*bekennende Kirche*), the movement that courageously placed itself in opposition to the church officially recognized by the Nazis, the "German Church" (*Deutsche Kirche*). Cf. Bethge, *Dietrich Bonhoeffer: Eine Biographie*, 870–71 (English translation: *Dietrich Bonhoeffer: A Biography*).

be regarded as an unethical act? It would seem that Bonhoeffer's course of action would imply an affirmative answer, but does that answer open the door to the kind of response that the Al-Qaida makes, viz, "The so-called civilized communities of the world have demonstrated that they are anti-Islam and morally bankrupt, so our own community bears the responsibility of fighting religious wars that strike at the centers of Evil like the World Trade Center Towers"? Viscerally, we answer no, but on what basis do we distinguish between Bonhoeffer's decision and the fanaticism and illusions of prophetic grandeur of Osama bin Laden? The answer is not one that can be facilely derived, for it lies at the heart of the covenantal bond intertwining the lives of people of faith with God's plan for the creation. Essential to that bond is the order upheld by moral principles. But the recital of the experiences of God's people in Scripture and subsequent history also testifies to horrendous events in which crazed individuals seized divine prerogatives and plotted to exterminate segments of God's family.

Bonhoeffer sought to understand the horrendous phenomenon of Hitler with appeal to a category ensconced in biblical tradition. In invoking the category of *Antichrist* to describe Hitler, Bonhoeffer was identifying the theological basis for his dread decision to seek the death of a fellow member of God's human family: Hitler had taken on the role of Satan in attacking and seeking to replace God's rule with his diabolical rule. If successful, he would undercut the moral foundation of the entire world, with a result of such cataclysmic dimensions as to be incalculable. Understood thus, Bonhoeffer's participation in the plot to assassinate Hitler can be seen as a profoundly moral act, albeit dreadful beyond imagining. It was an act neither arbitrarily chosen nor individually determined, but worked out, again to borrow a Kierkegaard's term, in "fear and trembling," but—and this is critically important—"fear and trembling" not in the heart of a lonely individual standing in solitude before a commanding God, but with fellow disciples within the covenantal context of "unlimited loyalty . . . under God."

Turning to earlier periods of American history, we find that the concept of covenant was frequently applied to politics. This was part of the more general tendency, from Puritan times on, for Americans to look to the Bible for political models. Already in the thirteen colonies, the influence of the concept of covenant, though variously construed, was pervasive. The Puritan leaders of Massachusetts and Connecticut, for example, whether magistrates or clergy, thought in terms of a covenant, established and maintained by God, as the framework for public life. Even when, as soon was the case, compromises had to be made in the moral and religious standards required for civic participation, these standards were construed in terms of covenant (e.g., "halfway covenant"). God, as Guarantor of the policies and laws that governed the Commonwealth, was the undisputed transcendent authority before whom oaths of loyalty were sworn, thus providing an ultimate grounding for political cohesion. Vestiges of this ultimate point of reference are still visible in the oaths generally taken over the Bible by witnesses in judicial courts and by elected and appointed officials upon being inaugurated into office, though that phenomenon when viewed in historical rather than ideological perspective suggests a much softer relation of national ethos to biblical epic than the more rigid theocratic perspective insisted upon by the Religious Right.[7]

Granting that from Puritan times political thought in the United States has been *influenced* by the biblical notion of covenant does not imply that covenant *fidelity* has shaped the history of the nation. Indeed, Robert Bellah traces the development of American civil religion under the heading of *The Broken Covenant*.[8] This provides an important reminder that lipservice to a covenantal understanding of public life does not in itself assure "unlimited loyalty" to truth-telling, justice, loyalty to one another, and indissoluble union. Intrinsic and essential to covenant as relationship is wholehearted

7. In an act reflective of increasing religious diversity, the first Muslim elected to the U.S. Congress, Keith Ellison, swore his oath of office over the Quran. Adding to the symbolic richness of the event was the fact that the copy of the Quran he used was from the library of Thomas Jefferson. Not surprisingly, the precedent set by Ellison drew sharp criticism from the representatives of the Religious Right such as *Townhall* columnist Dennis Prager, though it is interesting that little attention was paid when in 1997 Gordon Smith of Oregon chose the Book of Mormon for his swearing-in ceremony to the U.S. Senate.

8. Bellah, *Broken Covenant*.

consent committed to purging self of the ever-present weight of claims to personal and national special privilege. Accordingly, prophets—that is, watchers—who publicly decry instances of covenant violation, distortion, and perversion are an essential part of any society construing its essential identity in covenantal terms. Even in tracing the history of broken covenant, therefore, Bellah demonstrates the importance of that concept over the course of United States history, for the very fact that the jeremiads of Frederick Douglas and the sermons of Walter Rauschenbusch were intelligible to their reluctant, wayward listeners indicates that the benchmark for judging the faithfulness of the nation was associated in the minds of at least a broad cross-section of the populace with the notion of covenant fidelity.[9]

FROM COVENANTED COMMUNITY TO THE UNENCUMBERED SELF

In *Habits of the Heart*,[10] Bellah and his collaborators described a major paradigm shift in the way Americans viewed public life, one in which earlier loyalties to neighbors and the nation had yielded to an anti-communitarian individualism that stultified the sense of civic obligations tied to covenant. Arising out of the social upheavals of the late sixties and seventies was an understanding of the relation of the individual to the larger society that differed categorically from "unlimited loyalty, under God, . . . to one another." In the place of loyalty to others, commentators began to speak of the "unencumbered self."[11]

Like most cultural revolutions, the appearance of the autonomous individual did not burst upon the scene like a meteor in the night but was the outgrowth of seeds planted by the Renaissance and Reformation that reached fruition in the philosophical movements of the eighteenth and nineteenth centuries referred to as the Enlightenment. Characteristic of earlier medieval societies was

9. Ibid., 55–60.

10. Bellah et al., *Habits of the Heart*.

11. Sandel, "Procedural Republic and the Unencumbered Self."

a traditionalism enforced by the twin authorities of ecclesiastical miter and royal crown. Once these authorities were successfully challenged by religious reformers and regional princes, the traditional foundation for an authoritative, hierarchical polity crumbled, and the search for a new basis began. Appeal to divine revelation to settle political disputes had been brought into disrepute by religious factiousness and the wars that ensued. Hope for social harmony, therefore, came to focus on a new instrument for discovering the common good that presumably could reestablish social accord, an instrument that, unlike the implements utilized by theologians and kings, was allegedly shared by every fair-minded human being: namely, *reason*.

The effect of this enthronement of reason was to situate the human in place of God as the center of the political universe and the agent responsible for discovering the good and the right. Though traditionalists would seek to defend truth claims based on the authority of the Church, an increasingly influential intellectual class turned to their philosophers as the ones best qualified to guide human thought toward universally recognized standards of truth, a situation recalling the world of Plato and Aristotle. But as was the case in ancient Athens, the new custodians of public values disagreed among themselves regarding the foundation stones necessary for social stability and prosperity. By the late eighteenth and early nineteenth centuries, the battles among the philosophers resembled on an intellectual level the religious wars between regional princes of the previous two centuries. In one sense, Immanuel Kant can be viewed as a staunch defender of the idea that objective knowledge is possible and that one of the primary responsibilities of philosophy is to describe the universal categories that guide reasoned inquiry. But in another sense, Kant prepared the way for the impending assault on the concept of universal knowledge with his epistemological insight that the only access we have to objects is through our senses.[12] With their claim that in the pursuit of truth there exists no universally acknowledged basis upon which the inquirer can claim disinterested objectivity, the historicists would take the next step. Inevitably, one is guided by presuppositions, and presupposi-

12. Kant, *Critique of Pure Reason*, 82–83 [A 42–43, B 59–60].

tions, being historically conditioned, cannot lay claim to universal validity.

What followed could be called "the unraveling of the Enlightenment project." In his attack on the German Idealism associated with Hegel, Søren Kierkegaard repudiated attempts to establish a rational basis for a universal morality. In its place he advanced his existentialist position that, faced with the necessity of deciding between a purely self-centered aesthetic perception of life and an authentically moral way of living, the person of faith would give assent to the Christian way of life strictly as an act of *submission to God*.[13] By its very nature, he argued, faith renounces all external assurances, including those provided by rational argumentation. In "fear and trembling," the believer places trust in God alone, a unique Being separated from humans by an "infinite qualitative distinction" and thus utterly transcending rational categories.[14]

While Kierkegaard stands tall as a defender of the traditional values associated with classical Christianity, his move away from the rational defense of a universal morality to what has been designated *perspectivism* paved the way for a much more radical departure. While concurring with Kierkegaard's dethronement of reason as the basis for a universal understanding of the right and the good, Friedrich Nietzsche pointed to the arbitrariness of according a privileged status to traditional (i.e., Judeo-Christian) morality. The anti-foundational, subjectivist framework that Kierkegaard had introduced provided no basis for defense against the move to relocate the source of morality away from tradition to the individual human will. A new world had dawned in which individuals did not find their identity through conformity to the beliefs and values of the community into which they had been born but through the assertion of selfhood dedicated to the fulfillment of personal needs and desires. The "transvaluation of all values" that became a possibility within the context of this new outlook is evident in Nietzsche's scornful dismissal of traditional Judeo-Christian virtues as exemplifications

13. Kierkegaard, *Either/Or*, 2:170–73.

14. Kierkegaard, *Training in Christianity*, 139.

of weakness in contrast to the self-assertion of the Superman, whom he promoted as the paragon of the new elite humanity.[15]

Obviously, there are serious problems with the transmutations introduced by Nietzsche. The issue here, however, is the tenacity and historical influence of the conceptual world he helped to construct. In a sense, this world was the logical extension of the human-centeredness introduced by the Enlightenment. Values and their religious or philosophical warrants were no longer to be defined by tradition or by the community of which one was a part, but by the individual, as a utilitarian imperative of the exercise of his or her rights. Since place of privilege was categorically denied any specific ideology, a multiplicity of rivals made their debut, each contending for the approval of individual free agents: e.g., utilitarianism, Marxism, empiricism, and pragmatism. The free reign of the individual, however, soon became a scary dream rather than a comforting reality, as the actual rules of the new game accorded success to those wielding power, a cadre characteristically motivated more by their own self-aggrandizing schemes than by commitments to a better humanity. This set the stage for the tragic ironies of the first half of the twentieth century, in which theoretically unprecedented freedoms led to unprecedented assaults on human dignity in the form of ideologically driven world wars and genocides defended on the basis of subjectively discovered and solipsistically buttressed "absolute" truths defining humanity not in terms of inclusivity but racial purity and superiority.

The legacy of Nietzsche extended beyond the international chaos of the first half of the twentieth century to the "naked square" of the 1980s and 90s. The new economic and military hegemony that arose with the crumbling of the Soviet Union evoked triumphalistic rhetoric of a new world order. But what was the state of health of the communities loosely held together in the new aggre-

15. Nietzsche, "Genealogy of Morals." Nietzsche traced the roots of cowardly morality to the glorification of submission and weakness within the Jewish and Christian religions (645). A central strategy in his version of Romanticism was a return to the primal ethics born of "the will-to-power," a conception that set him on a collision course with the central beliefs of biblical covenantal thinking.

gate? At least in the Western nations that fell heir to the postmodern legacy, the source of values and morality of the masses got mired down in the solipsism of perspectivism, that is, in the murkiness of the individual will. Alastair MacIntyre has argued that this has led to a highly ambivalent situation in the ongoing search for the communal values that are still arguably necessary for the maintenance of a viable society.[16] Within the modern pluralistic society, traditional terms such as *liberty, freedom*, and *rights* continue to provide the vocabulary of moral reflection and political deliberation, but they bear widely divergent meanings derived from the highly personalistic perspectives that they have come to reflect. The result is a situation in which the parties participating in public debate fail to experience the kind of genuine communication that can lead to the resolution of conflicts, the negotiation of compromises, and the identification of mutually acceptable strategies for improving the commonweal.

From the social sciences, highly regarded savants such as Robert Bellah, Michael Sandel, and Robert Putman have sounded an alarm that all is not well with our democracy and the principles and procedures that guide it.[17] Like Alasdair MacIntyre, they have turned to the past for the lessons that can be found in the classics.[18] Two considerations commend an examination of the light that biblical tradition in particular can shed on the contemporary dilemma. First, the Bible is one of the classics of our civilization that continues to provoke lively discussion and command widespread respect. Second, the Bible contains profound insight into fundamental questions of governance that have not been adequately scrutinized. We turn, therefore, to explore further the contemporary significance of the Bible by examining in detail the concept of covenant in the message of the prophet Isaiah.

16. MacIntyre, *After Virtue*.
17. Sandel, *Democracy's Discontent*; Putnam, *Bowling Alone*.
18. See also Bloom, *The Closing of the American Mind*.

THE BACKGROUND OF ISAIAH'S COVENANTAL WORLDVIEW

A topic of lively debate among biblical scholars revolves around the question of whether the concept of "covenant" (ברית, *berith*) entered the religious thought-world of ancient Israel at an early or a later period. The long-standing view that covenant traditions trace back to the earliest stages of Israelite religion has been challenged in recent scholarship.[19] However, it is very difficult to explain how covenant came to play such a central role in the thought of the prophets and historians of the eighth and seventh centuries BCE without antecedents in earlier tradition. Part of the problem stems from imposition of the unjustifiably narrow linguistic perspective of limiting evidence exclusively to texts containing the term *berith*. Common sense would suggest that it is preferable to construe the matter substantively, by taking into consideration all traditions in which the *notion* of a covenantal relation between God and people forms an indispensable part of the conceptual background.[20] When the biblical evidence is approached from this broader perspective, the antiquity of the idea of covenant becomes apparent. From the earliest stages of Israelite history, the identity of the people was de-

19. E.g., Perlitt, *Bundestheologie im Alten Testament*; Thompson, *Early History of the Israelite People*; Thompson, *Bible in History*; Thompson, *Mythic Past*. Cf. McCarthy, *Treaty and Covenant*; and Nicholson, *God and His People*.

20. In innumerable texts containing reference to legal terms, such as תורה (*torah*), חקים (*huqim*), משפטים (*mišpaṭim*), and עדות (*'eduth*), a covenantal conceptual framework is assumed. In Hosea 8:10 and Psalm 78:10, the connection is made explicit through the parallel covenant/Torah. For an account of the development of covenantal thought in ancient Israel, see Hanson, *People Called*. The problem moves to another level, to be sure, if one accepts the radical revisionism of Thomas L. Thompson (see n. 19 above), who places the origin of the bulk of Israel's religious and historiographic traditions in Persian and Hellenistic times. This position is contradicted both by inner-biblical evidence and the witness of archaeological and extra-biblical epigraphic sources. McBride has formulated succinctly the position: "The covenant idea is ancient in Israel, underlying the centuries-long development of tradition that culminated in the reflective, comprehensive promulgation of a constitutional Torah during the later Judaean monarchy" ("Polity of the Covenant People, The Book of Deuteronomy," 237 n. 19).

rived from the notion that Israel's God, through actions on their behalf in history, had drawn them into a relationship based on commitments on both sides—that is to say, into *covenant*. This covenant provided the only dependable basis within the realms of commerce, government, the judiciary, and family life for truth-telling, justice, human loyalties, and indissoluble union.[21]

Visible throughout the history of biblical Israel are two aspects of covenant: covenant promises and covenant obligations.[22] The promises of prosperity, peace, and posterity rested solidly on the idea that the ultimate source of life was not the human agent, even as the tenacity of Israel's hope for restoration after calamity transcended human constraints and was based on belief in the dependability of a moral universe created and maintained by a faithful and purposeful God. But covenant promises were divorced from covenant obligations only at Israel's peril, for divine blessing was understood not mechanically but relationally. Blessing was conditional upon obedience; or better, the two were intrinsically connected, and if they were divided, the goal of covenant, namely, universal harmony (שלום, *šalôm*), disintegrated into chaos.[23] The vast architecture of Torah in the Hebrew Bible attests to the indispensable importance of covenant obligations. They were inextricably bound up with the

21. The location of the concept of covenant within ancient Israel's Near Eastern political/cultural setting has been elucidated by several groundbreaking works that retain their relevancy: Mendenhall, *Law and Covenant in Israel and the Ancient Near East*; Baltzer, *Covenant Formulary*; and Hillers, *Covenant*.

22. The mutuality involved in Israel's notion of covenant is expressed most succinctly in the formula "I shall be your God and you shall be my people" (see, for example, Exodus 6:7; Leviticus 26:12; Jeremiah 7:23; Ezekiel 36:28). The promise/obligation duality finds its clearest formulation in Deuteronomy 26:17-18: "Today you have obtained the LORD's agreement: to be your God . . . Today the LORD has obtained your agreement: . . . to keep his commandments" (all translations are from the NRSV).

23. Jeremiah 4 dramatically illustrates this covenantal pattern: The chapter begins with the plea of the Lord to the covenant partner, "If you return to me . . . ," but the condition of obedience upon which the covenant is based is repudiated by Israel (vv. 18–23), resulting in universal calamity: "I looked on the earth, and lo, it was waste and void; and to the heavens, and they had no light" (v. 23).

stability of the universe.[24] Maintenance of order accordingly entailed more than the pious individual conducting life on the basis of Torah. On a deeper level, those participating in God's covenant were partners maintaining a cosmic order. Awareness of this depth-structure of biblical ethics alone enables adequate understanding of the exception to general morality invoked by Bonhoeffer and the Confessing Church. The final location of the categorical imperatives defining universal morality is the universal rule of the Sovereign of the universe. Conventional day-to-day ethics must retain its normativity in the day-to-day, but norms regulating normalcy must not exclude exceptional measures when mandated by an assault on the entire world-order by Antichrist.

The eighth-century prophet Isaiah both inherited and enriched the Yahwistic worldview based on covenant. As was the case with Amos and Hosea, his indictments of the people are based on the obligations binding on the people as their side of the covenant traced to Moses.[25] Moreover, his view of a moral universe governed by divine retribution reflects traditional covenantal thought.[26] The theme of divine promise, which Isaiah upheld even in times of national peril, preserves the other dimension of the covenant formulary, now enriched by the covenant tradition associated with Jerusalem and the Davidic monarchy.[27]

COVENANT AS THE FOUNDATION FOR ISAIAH'S UNDERSTANDING OF REALITY

Above we suggested that it is necessary to go beyond a narrow study of the lexeme ברית (*berith*, "covenant") to a broader philological analysis of biblical traditions to understand the full significance of this notion in biblical thought. Specifically in the case of the eighth-century prophet Isaiah this broader approach is essential. In materi-

24. Hosea 4:1–3 illustrates this vividly, as does Isaiah 24:4–6.

25. Isaiah 3:13–15; 5:18–25; 10:1–4. Admonitions, such as Isaiah 1:16–17, also reflect Mosaic covenantal tradition.

26. Isaiah 29:20–21; 30:12–14.

27. Isaiah 1:19–20, 26; 30:18; 31:5.

als that confidently can be attributed to Isaiah, ברית occurs only in Isaiah 28:15, 18; and 33:8. It is found with considerably higher frequency in the exilic and postexilic portions of the Isaianic corpus (Isaiah 24:5; 42:6; 49:8; 54:10; 55:3; 56:4, 6; 59:21; 61:8). These portions reflect the thought of writers working within the conceptual world of Isaiah of Jerusalem and thus could be elicited as indirect evidence of the importance of covenantal thought in the "master teacher." However, I take the more conservative approach of confining our analysis to the portions of the book ascribable to the eighth-century prophet himself.[28] Focus on that message will reveal a thought-world founded solidly on the central tenets of covenant.

If Richard Niebuhr's pithy expression "unlimited loyalty . . . under God" captures the essence of a political understanding of covenant, the prophet Isaiah can be regarded as a staunch defender of a covenantal understanding of the life of his own nation. No prophet makes a clearer case for the twin biblical truths that there is no reality in the entire universe comparable with God and that the viability of a nation depends utterly upon conformity to the moral principles authored by this unique Being. We shall portray Isaiah's covenantal understanding of politics by sequentially examining his understanding of God and then his development of the relational concept of unlimited loyalty, for which he uses the term בטח (*bṭḥ*, "trust").

There is no epithet that better captures Isaiah's understanding of ultimate Reality than "Holy One of Israel" (קדוש ישראל, *qadoš yiśraʾel*). One of the cardinal teachings of biblical faith is the ineffable glory and uniqueness of the One who transcends all else. This teaching has found expression in formulations as diverse as Kierkegaard's

---

28. Such delimitation is not intended as a denial of the importance of studies that trace a concept throughout the book of Isaiah, for these studies have identified the threads of thought that tie together the canonical book of Isaiah as a unity. See, for example, Seitz, ed., *Reading and Preaching the Book of Isaiah*. Most recently, Fr. Leclerc has demonstrated how the concept of justice (משפט, *mišpaṭ*) was reapplied by each of the communities coming to articulation in the book of Isaiah to its particular situation, thereby illustrating the complementarity of continuity and change that is a mark of every dynamic religious tradition: Leclerc, *Yahweh Is Exalted in Justice*.

"infinite qualitative distinction" between God and humanity[29] and Rudolph Otto's *mysterium tremendum et fascinans*.[30] The 2500-year liturgical history of the Trisagion (based on Isaiah 6:3) suggests that Isaiah can be credited with giving classical formulation to the idea of God's holiness. The Trisagion reverberates from the scene depicting the prophet's encounter with God in an awesome, career-shaping experience that stamped his entire being with the only Reality that carried ultimate significance and that relativized all other loyalties at best to penultimacy. That experience enabled Isaiah to capture with unprecedented clarity an insight with roots reaching back to Israel's earliest confessions: there is only one political regime in the universe that is absolute and enduring, over against which the self-aggrandizing empires of the world are consigned to futility. Only through submission to the Holy One in trust, humility, and obedience is deliverance from this futility possible.[31]

We shall turn shortly to Isaiah's description of the nature of that submission, for it forms the basis of his construal of unlimited loyalty. But first we take note of one more detail in Isaiah's vision of the Holy One: the daunting, purging sense of awe before which the only fitting mortal response is the dread of "sinners in the hands of an angry God."[32] That experience carries Isaiah beyond a universal phenomenology of holiness to an awareness of the connection between the high and lofty Sovereign of the universe and his own nation. God is revealed as the Holy One of *Israel*.[33] Out of his experience of dread before the Holy One, Isaiah confesses his solidarity with a specific *people* (Isaiah 6:5), and once he has been absolved of his sin he hears the LORD directing him back to that same people (v. 9). The message he is given in vv. 9–13 seems to consign the nation to doom and can be understood aright only with reference to the profound influence Isaiah's concept of divine holiness has on

29. Kierkegaard, *Training in Christianity*, 139.

30. Otto, *Idea of the Holy*.

31. Cf. Exodus 15:11; Judges 5:3–5, 31; 8:22–23.

32. This vivid phrase is borrowed from the title of a sermon delivered by Jonathan Edwards in Enfield, Connecticut, in 1741.

33. Cf. Roberts, "Isaiah in Old Testament Theology," esp. 68–71.

his political understanding. For the one enveloped by the numinous terror of the Holy One, the very possibility of anything human surviving the purging effects of God's holiness is called into question. This primal sense of awe that infuses Isaiah's entire message must be held in mind as we turn to the second pillar of Isaiah's political understanding. The only viable framework for the possibility of nationhood is a relationship solely based on divine grace and strictly conditional on the human response of unlimited loyalty expressed in obedience to the will of God.[34] No single word expresses this relationship more precisely than "covenant." We turn now to describe the response called for from the human partner in the covenant.

The word Isaiah uses to express the fitting human response is "trust" (בטח, *bth*), a word that carries all of the connotations of Niebuhr's phrase "unlimited loyalty." In a covenantal understanding of nationhood, citizens express their loyalty to their government in the first instance through acknowledgment of its utter dependence on the Ruler of all peoples and the Creator of the universe. The authentic patriot reserves ultimate loyalty for God alone and is thus freed from the slavery of nationalistic idolatry and purified to contribute to the health of the body politic.

In describing the fitting response of humans to the Holy One, Isaiah once again draws upon the tradition of his people. He describes the notion of covenant, not abstractly, but in terms of the relationship between God and a particular people. Just so, the terms of trust and unlimited loyalty are not left as theoretical constructs but exposited in the form of explicit commandments arising out of Israel's history with their God and applying to the concrete realities of day-to-day existence.[35] For Isaiah, as for his fellow prophets,

34. Eichrodt expressed Israel's relationship to God thus: "The nation thus chosen is protected by a power above all other powers in the world, but is constantly answerable to its demands in the world and must follow them unconditionally"; Eichrodt, "Prophet and Covenant," 170.

35. Isaiah relates to the Torah tradition of his community in the same manner as his contemporary Micah: "[God] has told you, O mortal, what is good; and what does the Lord require of you but to do justice, and to love kindness, and to walk humbly with your God?" (Micah 6:8). For anyone with an open mind and heart, the conditions of the covenant are self-evident. Isaiah is baffled that a people that has received such clear testimony of both God's

the community living in trust of God expresses its loyalty in two ways: in worship, through which it renews its communion with its Source; and in obedience to the commandments, in which it aligns itself with the universal moral order established by God. Worship and obedience constitute an indivisible unity, as Isaiah's condemnation of "solemn assemblies with iniquity" makes clear (Isaiah 1:14). Together, worship and obedience safeguard the life and foster the blessings that constitute *shalom*: that is, the harmony intended by God for all creation. In sum, Isaiah's covenantal view of reality is an interactive, relational view, in which all players have assigned responsibilities that if discharged properly uphold the human side of the covenant and provide the foundation for national well-being.

Israel's rebellion against God contradicts even the natural law that Isaiah sees manifested in the world of beasts (Isaiah 1:3). Still, the persistent resistance to Isaiah's message from Israel's religious and political leaders forces him to face head-on the sobering subtheme that accompanies the religious traditions to which he fell heir: since humans possess the freedom either to accept or to reject their Creator and Redeemer, life in covenant entails a perennial struggle. The tragedy that enshrouds human history arises from the common pattern of mortals claiming autonomy and self-rule, resulting in the chaos of each living for personal gain and treating others not as kinsfolk but as competitors in a zero-sum game. It is this subtheme that contributes a distinctly somber note to Isaiah's politics. It accounts for the earnestness with which he approaches the subject of governance. We turn now to his own words and actions to see how his covenantal understanding of national life, while deeply indebted to the religious traditions of his people, was given a new focus and a sense of urgency through his personal experiences.

---

mercy on its behalf and God's requirements could persist in rebellion. He reaches to the realm commonly associated with wisdom literature, the realm of nature, to document the absurdity of Israel's position: "The ox knows its owner, and the donkey its master's crib; but Israel does not know, my people do not understand" (Isaiah 1:3).

THE POLITICS OF ISAIAH IN PRACTICE

Divine Government

Isaiah's profound personal encounter with the Holy One of Israel added poignancy to the truth to which he as a prophet had fallen heir, regarding the indispensable connection between human politics and theo-politics—that is, God's governance of the universe. The first principle of national life is that it exists under the rule of God; to ignore this is, for Isaiah, equivalent to a pronouncement of doom. The nation that ignores or repudiates the sole claim of God to ultimate loyalty inevitably falls prey to hubris and consequently to its own undoing. Political and religious leaders, such as those who ridiculed Isaiah's calls to submission before the Holy One and maintained their self-originating authority,[36] nullified their legitimacy and were declared by the prophet to be enemies of the very people they claimed the right to rule. The starting point in tracing the contours of Isaiah's politics is therefore a glance at his understanding of divine government as the only regime worthy of the unconditional loyalty of the people, which understanding alone could place upon a firm foundation the legitimacy and integrity of dependable human government.

It is not an exaggeration to regard as one of the most significant contributions of Israel's prophetic tradition to political theory the distinction between the two loyalties required of every citizen—ultimate loyalty to God and penultimate loyalty to a lawfully instituted human regime. This principle appears to have arisen in ancient Israel out of the struggles to fashion a new form of kingship. The wisest of Israel's religious sages during the monarchy acknowledged the need for a centralized government at the same time as they insisted that safeguards had to be built into the nation's laws and institutions capable of preserving the essential moral values that constituted the heart of Israel's epic, the centerpiece of which was that epic's confession that Yahweh was a God of mercy. Coming to expression repeatedly in the Torah was the confession that divine

---

36. E.g., Isaiah 30:8–14.

mercy was manifested especially in protecting and empowering the weak and enslaved. Therefore, it comes as no surprise that the elevation of one human to a status of special privilege and worth—a central tenet of royal ideology—would give rise to serious tensions. According to the narrative in 1 Samuel 7, Israel's last judge threw down the gauntlet: adoption of kingship would place strict limits on the freedoms that were taken for granted under tribal rule. To a people awakening to the liabilities of the new form of government, Samuel explained that their only hope rested in recognizing the crucial distinction between ultimate and penultimate loyalty (1 Samuel 12:19–25). Fear and worship as forms of unconditional loyalty were to be reserved for God alone. Otherwise, both king and people were doomed. In Deuteronomy 17:14–20, this prophetic principle was codified: in Israel, the king. no less than any ordinary citizen, was bound by the conditions of the Torah.

The categorical distinction between two levels of government was a principle that Isaiah inherited from his ancestral faith. But it is evident from the message that he directed to the governing and governed of his time that he had grasped the critical importance of this principle with a clarity and urgency that is unique in the Hebrew Bible. Isaiah's personal, foundation-shaking encounter with the Holy One of Israel (described in Isaiah 6) clarified the significance of that principle. That encounter also propelled him, with a sense of life-and-death urgency, to bring God's sovereignty to the attention of his people in a last-ditch effort to snatch Israel from the brink of national calamity.

At the heart of Isaiah's politics is a vision of reality that defines a distinct theology, anthropology, and political science. It contains the radical claim that failure to recognize that every human government stands under the authority, scrutiny, and judgment of divine government is tantamount to political suicide. The state that falls into the delusion of grandeur that has characterized all of the mighty empires of the past will suffer their ignoble fate. From an Isaianic perspective, the religious leader's potential to lead his or her country is contingent on the clear understanding that human government is legitimate only as an agent of the universal rule of One who transcends all regional and national self-interest. Once all earthly power becomes relativized before the Holy One, a basis is established for determining goals and priorities in the political realm without the distraction of matters that carry no ultimate validity:

> Holy, holy, holy is the LORD of hosts;
> the whole earth is full of his glory. (Isaiah 6:3)

In words reverberating with numinous power, the Trisagion gives classical expression to the central truth that Isaiah inherited from early Yahwism and to which he contributed significantly through his own courageous testimony. Only in the presence of the Holy One does the human find his/her authentic identity, and this discovery's first moment is the experience of abject unworthiness: "Woe is me! I am lost, for I am a man of unclean lips, and I live among a people of unclean lips; yet my eyes have seen the King, the LORD of hosts!" (Isaiah 6:5). This defines the central tenet of the covenantal relationship: all of life is to be ordered on the basis of unconditional loyalty to the Holy One. God alone can draw errant humans into a community that assures the dignity of every individual and fosters in an uncompromising inclusiveness the well-being of all members, from the most humble peasant to the highest echelons of religious and political leadership.

"Woe is me," to be sure, is unlikely any time soon to become the slogan of a political party. It does not comport with the androcentric, emotivistic perspectivism that we described earlier as characterizing the modern self-consciousness. Nietzsche, in fact, could cite it as an example of the pathetic frailty of the biblical concept of the human. The theo-politics of Isaiah, if taken seriously today, thus represents a fundamental challenge to prevailing assumptions. For Isaiah presented the audacious view that submission before a Reality that transcends all human authority was the only option capable of stemming the disintegration of civil life into chaos (Isaiah 3:1–8). Does such a view have any chance of being heeded in a world infatuated with the notion of autonomous human agency?

Isaiah would answer thus (and Reinhold Niebuhr would agree): Only when all created beings are relativized under the ineffable transcendent One, who is immune to manipulation and favoritism, can a government be established in which equality and truth-telling in relationships can be preserved. Where associations are formed in acknowledgment of the ultimate rule of the Holy One, commitments to the terms of the charter are not contingent on pragmatic considerations, such as the enhancement of benefits to some at the cost of others or compromises predicated on the avoidance of inconvenience. In a culture given to capricious associations—or, to use the phrase of a John Winthrop House student quoted in the Harvard student daily, *The Crimson*, "hot, mad hookups"—covenantal language may sound rigid. But, far from fostering inflexibility, it provides the only authentic basis for relationships that are dependable and enduring. The alternative to unconditional truthfulness, under God, is the murky flux of unpredictability and whim that leads to discord and finally to civil chaos. Rules no longer are respected, and politics becomes a battlefield in which outcomes are determined by force rather than civil debate, persuasion, and open elections.[37]

By starting with divine government as the sole basis for legitimate human government, Isaiah envisions a moral order according to which institutions predicated on claims to special privilege and buttressed by the accumulation of wealth and power are nullified. In instances of the violation of the intrinsic dignity of an individual, the victim has recourse to the Holy One, before whom all distinctions dissolve.[38] As for enforcement, Isaiah is emphatic that acts of breaking covenantal commitments inevitably lead to corrective consequences. Isaiah is realistic in his awareness that the ambiguities of human existence entail delays in retributive corrections, but he never doubts that God's universal order of even-handed justice ultimately will prevail over every alternative human construal of government.

37. The history of modern Afghanistan may serve as illustration of this point, where regimes have been deposed and replaced in rapid succession by the force of arms rather than through elections reflecting the will of the people. At the same time, certain irregularities in the U.S. presidential election of November 7, 2000, caution against self-righteous, nationalistic smugness.

38. The intimate bond between divine majesty and justice is expressed succinctly in Isaiah 5:16b: "the Holy God shows himself holy by righteousness." According to Isaiah 29:23–24, the inextricable tie between worship and *torah* will be understood on the day that the people at last understand the essential truth lying at the heart of their religious tradition.

While Isaiah looks to God as the final arbiter of justice and is unswerving in his trust in the God who finally will inaugurate a lasting reign of peace,[39] his response to the abuses he witnesses in his nation is not limited to an eschatological vision of final vindication. It is clear that his trust in God and his loyalty to God's universal moral order direct his attention incisively toward every instance of corruption and abuse of power that he sees in the immediate world around him. The competing system of governance based on the privileged status and entitlement of the powerful elite represents an affront to the Holy One and comes under wilting condemnation:

> Ah, you who join house to house,
>   who add field to field,
> until there is room for no one but you ...
> The LORD of hosts has sworn in my hearing:
> Surely many houses shall be desolate,
>   large and beautiful houses, without inhabitant. (Isaiah 5:8–9)

Though this pronouncement may at first appear to reflect a mechanistic understanding of retribution, closer scrutiny reveals that it arises out of the intricately relational universe of Isaiah's theo-politics. In this universe, everything depends ultimately on the nature of the deity, for if the divine government were capricious in the manner of the Olympian gods, anomie would not be obviated but rather elevated to a higher estate. The significance of the fact that Isaiah's favorite epithet for God is "Holy One" is thus manifest: The holy God, as the ultimate source of just government, is not an abstract philosophical construction, but an experienced, living Reality, both exalted above the heavens and inscribed on the heart of every creature. By applying divine justice to everyday economics and political policy, Isaiah is remaining true to the epic tradition of his ancestral faith. According to that tradition, the God of mercy and righteousness was not a theoretical concept confined to discussions among the sages, but the living Reality already experienced by Israel's oppressed ancestors in the Egyptian slave compounds. There, humans

39. E.g., Isaiah 2:2–4. The "Isaianic School" faithfully cultivated the eschatological vision of *shalom*), as seen in Isaiah 35:1–10; 42:1–4; 61:1–4; and 65:17–25.

whose integrity had been violated and desecrated found themselves drawn into the custody of a merciful and just Deliverer. In this ancient epic, the emerging community therefore confessed that the God of the universe, awesome in holiness, is a God who reaches out in mercy to restore the broken, deliver the oppressed, and thwart the schemes of the wicked.[40]

Out of this epic emerged the contours of divine government that Isaiah reiterates and then applies to the day-to-day realities of the human government under which he lives.

Having located the basis of Isaiah's political thought in the notion of divine government, we turn to describe the nature of his engagement with the structures of governance of his time. Though frequently in history theo-politics has led to passivity, Isaiah, on the basis of his belief that God enlists those faithful to the covenant as partners in the extension of divine order to the orders of human existence, demonstrates a style of participation in political process that is proactive, consistent, and courageous.

Human Government

How does Isaiah understand and deal with human government? The most obvious evidence that God's universal *imperium* leaves room for human participation in the form of human government is the widespread phenomenon of misgovernment. Although divine rule is the ultimate source of human government, the widespread

---

40. Though Isaiah's own experience of God as a holy Presence added a deeply personal dimension to his reforming zeal, it would be false to construe his moral principles in subjective terms. His position is as far removed from what we described above as "emotivism" as can be imagined. For Isaiah, the fact that God was a God showing mercy to and empowering the weak was a truth ensconced in Israel's religious epic. That humans in turn were to practice mercy and justice even-handedly and without regard to human categories of status was an incontestable truth, preserved in the Torah and required of every mortal categorically. If the ideals of justice and mercy were repudiated, dire consequences would ensue (Isaiah 5:7; the woes that follow in 5:8-30 and 10:1-11 vividly describe the violations of God's commands and the consequences; 1:19-20 gives the abbreviated version of crime and punishment).

instances of regimes that repudiate the commandments of the Holy One by devoting worship to nationalistic idols and political policy to the enrichment of the privileged elite prove that God does not impose his rule over passive human beings. In three passages (Isaiah 9, 11, and 2), the prophet gives eloquent descriptions of the qualities of human government that are in harmony with God's universal rule. The background of Isaiah 9 is the kind of political disorder all too common in human history. Oppression, violence, and the devastation of war bear down on the governed (9:2–5). Reflecting the common Near Eastern practice of his time of conferring upon the king multiple throne names,[41] the prophet announces the qualities that will enable the coming ruler to succeed: "Wonderful Counselor, Mighty God, Everlasting Father, Prince of Peace" (9:6). In contrast to the preceding chaos, the new government will cultivate "enduring *shalom.*" The foundation for this *shalom* is delineated, and then its source is revealed:

> He will establish and uphold it with justice and with righteousness
> from this time onward and forevermore.
> The zeal of the LORD of hosts will do this. (Isaiah 9:7b)

The human ruler is equipped with extraordinary qualities, but ultimately, the success of his rule can be established solely by the support of the heavenly Ruler.

In Isaiah 11, the prophet returns to the theme of human government, again emphasizing source and qualities. This time the source is described in terms of "the spirit of the LORD" (Isaiah 11:2a). This notion becomes central in later biblical and post-biblical understandings of the way that God is experienced within the human community and the way that human polities can receive direction in the manner of government that conforms to divine will. The leadership qualities conferred by the spirit of the Lord provide a remarkable profile of the nature of proper human government: "wisdom and understanding," "counsel and might," "knowledge and

---

41. Frankfort, *Kingship and the Gods*, 46–47. For further literature on the subject of the Egyptian background of the royal titles in Isaiah 9:5b, see Wildberger, *Isaiah 1–12*, 402. The attribution of lofty titles to Babylonian and neo-Assyrian kings like Hammurabi and Sennacherib is also well attested.

the fear of the LORD" (11:2). Most remarkable of all is the identification of the motivational core that integrates all of these qualities into a dynamic unity: "His delight shall be in the fear of the LORD" (11:3a). The purpose behind this leader is not personal gain or power. Political leadership is recognized as energized by "counsel and might," but these qualities that are so vulnerable to personal aggrandizement are purified by submission to the Lord.

The portrait of government and its leadership is so bright in the above two passages as to raise the question of what has come of the somber realism present in so many other utterances of the Isaiah. Has something led to his abandoning the common biblical view stated succinctly by Jeremiah, that "the heart is devious above all else" (Jeremiah 17:9)? Far from the ebullient view of the future found in Isaiah 9 and 11, the more sober biblical anthropology could be expected to lead to a political philosophy along the following lines: God does not rule directly; humans mediate, but humans are devious; *ergo*, the thought of just human government is illusory. Isaiah avoids this counsel of despair by carefully drawing an important distinction:

> He shall not judge by what his eyes see,
>> or decide by what his ears hear;
> but with righteousness he shall judge the poor,
>> and decide with equity for the meek of the earth.
> (Isaiah 11:3b–4a)

Plainly, the ruler appeals to something beyond personal opinion, but what is that something, and can it be trusted? Righteousness (צֶדֶק, *ṣedeq*) and equity (מִישׁוֹר, *mîšôr*) constitute a hendiadys referring to the cumulative moral wisdom embodied in Israel's spiritual legacy, the Torah. The structures of government that maintain the corporate life of this people will conform to divine government if they embody the ethical ideals that were shaped by Israel's history with the God of righteous compassion as framed in the epic and codified in the Torah.

> Righteousness shall be the belt around his waist,
>> and faithfulness the belt around his loins. (11:5)

Isaiah rests his confidence, accordingly, on his religious community's normative traditions, because he recognizes their ultimate source in the Holy One.

Finally, in chapter 2 Isaiah lifts his sight even higher toward an eschatological vision of the time when his nation would fulfill its true vocation as agent of God's *torah* and thus prepare for a world living in righteousness and peace. Unlike the great empires of Egypt and Assyria, Israel's national destiny was not to be construed in terms of an imperialism buttressed by military might and the export of weapons. Far from being known for its war colleges, Jerusalem would be sought out for instruction in how to convert armaments into instruments of peace, to the end that "nation shall not lift up sword against nation, neither shall they learn war any more" (2:4b).

At the same time that Isaiah is eloquent in his description of good government, he is soberly realistic about the impediments that lead to the tragic history of conflict between nations and the incalculable harm thereby inflicted upon their citizens. Here too his analysis is based on the relationship between human and divine government. Whereas the proper relation can be summarized by trust and obedience, the perversion of the covenantal relationship takes the form of prideful self-assertion. Isaiah is unrelenting in his denunciation of human pride, which one can understand best by reference to his experience of the Holy One. Once one's eyes have been opened to the majesty of God, human pride becomes a farce. Whether displayed by an Assyrian emperor laying claim to divine status (Isaiah 14:12–20), the wealthy trader luxuriating in gain accumulated at the expense of the poor (10:1–4), the courtesan flaunting her finery and jewels (3:16–26), or the political leader or judge using public office as an opportunity to rob the people (29:20–21), human pride is an absurdity deserving of ridicule and scorn.

Though Isaiah does not aspire to the role of king, judge, or priest, he takes very seriously the theo-political office to which he has been commissioned by God, one requiring him to remind political and religious leaders alike of the essential relation between human government and divine rule. We shall complete our examination of Isaiah's politics by citing one case from each of the files included in his portfolio: the domestic, the international, and the religious.

We turn first to Isaiah 3:14–15 as an example of Isaiah's critique of his nation's *domestic policy*:

> The LORD enters into judgment
>> with the elders and princes of his people;
> "It is you who have devoured the vineyard;
>> the spoil of the poor is in your houses.
> What do you mean by crushing my people,
>> by grinding the face of the poor?
> says the Lord GOD of Hosts.

The seriousness of such perversion of political responsibility for the polis is recognized only if one recognizes the relation of human government to divine rule. Against this background, what may on the surface appear to be petty political corruption, or even possession on the basis of eminent domain, is unmasked as an assault on the sacred order that defends the dignity and security of every citizen against all forms of oppression. For this reason, the distinction that we draw between domestic and foreign policy, while heuristically useful, is morally epiphenomenal. The security of Jerusalem rests much more on the moral armament manifested in showing mercy and doing justice than on military might.

A vivid example of Isaiah's application of covenantal politics to *international affairs* is found in chapters 7–8. First, a word of background: The prophet's nation, Judah, was engulfed by an international crisis in 734 BCE. Under siege by the armies of Syria and Judah's sister state, Israel, pressure was building for King Ahaz to take the expedient route of allying with Assyria, which, according to the conventions of ancient Near Eastern treaties, entailed official acknowledgment of the Assyrian deities. Rather than laying out the details of foreign policy, Isaiah points to the bearing of divine government on the situation. To the king he announces, "If you do not stand firm in faith, you shall not stand at all" (7:9b). Unmistakable are the twin pillars of Isaiah's theo-politics: "under God/unlimited loyalty." In a similar crisis thirty years later, he offers a similar word:

> In returning and rest you shall be saved;
>> in quietness and in trust shall be your strength." (30:15)

The position taken by Isaiah in the face of a daunting military crisis is understood by many (including my colleague Lawrence Stager) as equivalent to the proverbial ostrich burying its head in the sand. Or does it embody a profound perspective on international policy that alone promises to arrest the tragic pattern of spiraling violence that spans human history? The one who shares Isaiah's vantage point of trust in God will conclude that it is the latter; that is, human government can succeed only if it is patterned after the qualities of divine government. In regard to international policy, this means that a nation's strength can be built and sustained only upon a moral foundation consisting of humility and dedication to compassionate justice. A nation guided by such principles will not panic in crisis but will work out its policy "in quietness and trust" so as to assure that it conforms to the righteous compassion for all creatures of all nations that is the cornerstone of God's universal rule. For, "if you do not stand firm in faith, you shall not stand at all."

Remembering that Isaiah, in keeping with his ancestral heritage, embraced worship and obedience as the twin responses that were entailed by covenant fidelity, we ask, finally, how did he view the relation of *religious institutions* to national health? Applied to Isaiah's situation, the question can be formulated thus: "What was the Lord's response to prideful politicians and aggressive traders flocking to religious festivals to thank God for their power and wealth?" The answer Isaiah receives is this:

> I cannot endure solemn assemblies with iniquity . . .
>
> [E]ven though you make many prayers, 1 will not listen;
> > your hands are full of blood.
> Wash yourselves; make yourselves clean;
> > remove the evil of your doings from before my eyes;
> cease to do evil,
> > learn to do good;
> seek justice,
> > rescue the oppressed,
> defend the orphan,
> > plead for the widow. (Isaiah 1:13b, 15b–17)

Isaiah's answer is unequivocal: religion apart from dedication to social justice represents the culminating mockery of the Holy One.

ISRAEL'S CHOICE: COVENANT WITH THE HOLY ONE OR COVENANT WITH DEATH

In spite of the eloquence with which Isaiah was able to describe the ideals of righteous government, it is evident that he at times viewed the political state of his nation as virtually hopeless. How else can we comprehend these words deriving from his inaugural encounter with the Holy One?

> "Keep listening, but do not comprehend;
>   keep looking, but do not understand."
> Make the mind of this people dull,
>   and stop their ears, and shut their eyes . . ." (Isaiah 6:9–10a)

Our initial response is that Isaiah is excessively pessimistic. But can we expect a cheerful message from one who seeks to call his people to their spiritual roots only to be meet with this rebuff?

> Do not prophesy to us what is right;
> speak to us smooth things,
>   prophesy illusions, . . .
> let us hear no more about the Holy One of Israel. (30:10, 11b)

The message that Isaiah has presented concerning submission and unlimited loyalty to the Holy One cuts to the heart of what the corrupt politicians, greedy merchants, and self-serving priests held most dear: their own comfort and power, regardless of the ensuing devastating impact on their subjects (10:1–2).

Sarcasm permeates this passage, but the theme it develops is utterly consistent with Isaiah's covenantal view. The conceptual house the people live in is a prison, because they have utterly distorted reality and now believe in their own lie:

> You turn things upside down!
>   Shall the potter be regarded as the clay?
> Shall the thing made say of its maker,
>   "He did not make me";
> or the thing formed say of the one who formed it,
>   "He has no understanding"? (29:16)

THE CHOICE BETWEEN COVENANTS: YAHWEH OR SHEOL

We can summarize Isaiah's fundamental message best by returning explicitly to the theme of covenant, the construal of reality that
insists that human government can be authentic and viable only if
it situates itself in the right relation to divine government. Here is
Isaiah's commentary on his nation's understanding of covenant:

> Therefore hear the word of the LORD, you scoffers
>   who rule this people in Jerusalem.
> Because you have said, "We have made a covenant with death,
>   and with Sheol we have an agreement;
> when the overwhelming scourge passes through
>   it will not come to us;
> for we have made lies our refuge,
>   and in falsehood we have taken shelter";
> therefore thus says the Lord GOD,
> See, I am laying in Zion a foundation stone,
>   a tested stone,
> a precious cornerstone, a sure foundation:
>   "One who trusts will not panic."
> And I will make justice the line,
>   and righteousness the plummet. (Isaiah 28:14–17a)

Once again, we encounter Isaiah as a master craftsman of
sarcasm. But his rhetoric remains strictly committed to a central
point. Three times in the immediate context,[42] all of them like the
present case relating to the international crisis of 705–701 BCE,
the prophet has attacked his nation's policy of pinning security to a
buildup of armaments rather than to "look to the Holy One of Israel
or consult the LORD" (31:1b). In this passage, the prophet unmasks
the national stratagem for what it is on an ultimate level, namely,
basing the nation's defense on an alliance with the chthonic forces
of the netherworld in repudiation of the living God. The effect is
the opposite of what is sought: Israel's leaders are ascending not to
the invincibility and immortality they believe can be delivered by
the pagan exercises of the fertility cults in which they indulge, but

---

42. Isaiah 30:1–5, 16–17; 31:1–3.

they are cascading willy-nilly into the doom and darkness of the hungry realm of Sheol, a realm that Isaiah described graphically in 5:14 (cf. Job 18:13). Even as the prophet earlier had drawn upon mythic motifs to warn of the consequences of a treaty entanglement with Assyria (Isaiah 8:5–8), so too in 28:14–17 he alludes to Canaanite lore to decry international policy that not only flies in the face of sound military judgment but represents a frontal attack on the only One capable of providing security for the nation. Isaiah thus remains consistent with his major premise, namely, that all the military might of the world cannot challenge the cosmic government that embraces all nations, all classes, all beings everywhere and for eternity. In contrast with government predicated on human pride, the prophet sets an alternative: government based on, to quote the prophet, "a sure foundation: 'One who trusts will not panic'" (28:16).

ISAIAH'S COVENANTAL POLITICS AND THE CONTEMPORARY WORLD

We began by describing a society that has renounced communal solidarity by ensconcing individualism and abjured deference to a legacy of shared values and moral principles in favor of an emotivism that establishes value on the basis of individual rights and benefits. In normal times, I could imagine our citizens continuing in this direction—little islands isolated from one another, each pursuing his or her own petty objectives in life, accumulating, consuming, and then dying, alone, and without connections, whether to each other, the past, the future, or to other peoples and cultures. But since September 11, 2001, these have not been normal times. Or, perhaps, these *are* normal times, in the sense that we have been thrust into solidarity with common humanity, where security and plenty cannot be taken for granted and where illness and unsatisfied hunger are routine. At any rate, we are facing a world in which individuals committed to decency and opposed to all that is vile—such as using passenger planes as bombs and fighter bombers as instruments to tear apart peasant villages—need to develop procedures for clarifying goals and defining ways to redress gross injustices and to restore human dignity to persons in all parts of the world. We begin to see signs of a willingness on the part of average folk to reengage in politics, to dedicate themselves to political change, to work for a more human society and a more equitable world.

In a complicated and dangerous times, goals and strategies for reaching them depend on more than agreements and contracts. They are too anemic. A world that is both in crisis and longing for new leadership needs to reconsider the lost values lying at the heart of *covenant*. In the wake of world wars, regional wars, and now wars no longer defined by battle-lines, humans can unite in cooperative endeavors only if they find a means of transcending their selfish, personalistic objectives, whether as individuals or nations.[43] In order to address questions of the decay of our environment, world hunger, ethnic and religious conflict, and economic profiteering, cooperative arrangements must be established that are committed to the principles of equality, freedom, and dignity for all.

In the present search for direction, the prophetic concept of covenant employed by Isaiah deserves renewed scrutiny. For it relates regional politics to cosmic politics and relativizes all parochial strategies by reference to one universal vision of justice, equality, and shared well-being. World history is littered with regional ideologies exploiting universal religious claims to advance their own imperialistic causes. For this, the prophet offers an enigmatic but poignant reply: religious communities must be able to distinguish between covenants of life and covenants of death. And governments must repudiate the temptation to use religion for their self-aggrandizing purposes and expose themselves to the watchful eyes of the prophets in their midst.

But, on what basis can such distinctions be made? Isaiah relied on the religious heritage of his people, a heritage that spoke of a God who created all peoples and who paid special attention to humans who were enslaved, impoverished, and denied the protection of loving community. It is in keeping with the dynamism of biblical tradition to affirm that every generation seek the wisdom of its prophets to formulate anew the distinction between the covenant of life and

43. Niebuhr, "Idea of Covenant," 135.

the covenant of death. A common response in our world, however, is to banish the concept of covenant, the notion of a transcendent order as the reference point for human government; or, stated from a religious perspective, of recourse to a transcendent Being as judge of every human being. The humanistic challenge is formidable. Myriad are the human tragedies that have been caused by ruthless tyrants claiming divine sponsorship. The arguments raised against theo-politics—that is, the application of religious beliefs and values to world problems—are weighty and demand the careful scrutiny of all theists.

However, the secular option, especially given the contemporary collapse of communalism into solipsism and emotivism, normally results in the Machiavellian world of policy determined by power. We must ponder, therefore, whether the wisdom of our ancient scriptural tradition may still be valid, perhaps even critically important. According to that wisdom, human governments and the populations they rule can prosper only if they acknowledge that they are not self-legitimizing but gain their legitimacy solely by conformity to a universal order that encompasses all living beings with even-handed justice and mercy.

At 9:00 a.m., Eastern Standard Time, on September 11, 2001, a society awoke to a reality that, though vivid in the minds of the citizens of Hiroshima, Hanoi, and Darfur, seemed distant from their own shores. Under a sun darkened by the billowing smoke pouring from the World Trade Center, they stared into the face of a world reeling out of control, a world captured in the haunting words of William Butler Yeats' "The Second Coming":

> Things fall apart; the centre cannot hold;
> Mere anarchy is loosed upon the world,
> The blood-dimmed tide is loosed, and everywhere
> The ceremony of innocence is drowned;
> The best lack all conviction, while the worst
> Are full of passionate intensity.

I should like to conclude this chapter by formulating the challenge we face as a society snatched by tragedy out of a history of isolated complacency and offered membership in the global community: Can a reliable foundation be built that will forestall atomistic disintegration? That depends on whether we can rediscover a framework for morally grounded political discourse that is capable of envisioning the goals of a humane society and world and defining the values needed to reach them. Communities of faith can add richness and depth to this challenging process, not the least by stressing the importance of affirming that the ultimate reference point for identifying the right and the good transcends every human institution. That the reference point is an elusive one faith communities will not deny, but rather embrace in humility and awe out of the depths of encounter with the Holy One in their own sacred traditions and ongoing communal experiences. Granted, many denounce the very concept of transcendence on the basis of all-too-frequent instances of its co-option by those who degrade religious traditions into serving their own self-aggrandizing or, in some cases even pathological, purposes. To them, we can commend consideration of another possibility, ever fragile, often broken, but not absent from the history of humankind: religious communities that trust and are guided by wise, compassionate leaders who embody the time-tested truths of sacred tradition and who do not shelter those truths from the purifying embers of other living faiths. The community that is still instructed by the moral insights of Richard Niebuhr and continues to follow in the path of the ancient prophets will remain loyal to the God who not only created but lovingly cares for all creatures. Such a community will find the fitting faith response in this time to be a simultaneous commitment to draw deeply and "in quietness and trust" on its own faith tradition and to remain open to the insights of the sages of all faiths regarding the nurturance of universal *shalom* as the destiny toward which the entire cosmos yearns.[44] To

44. One example of the effect of interreligious dialogue is the reexamination of many of their teachings that Christians have undertaken as the result of the truth-telling of Muslims and Jews regarding the vile assaults on human dignity in the Crusades and the Holocaust. Examples could be added from other religious communities but the main point should be clear: All of the great world religions rightly understood, point beyond natural parochial concerns and prejudices to visions of universal harmony, and therefore they all stand to benefit from lively interreligious dialogue as well as cooperative efforts on behalf of peace and justice.

respond thus is to renounce every covenant with death and to embrace wholeheartedly the covenant of life in a form that meets the weighty challenges of our present age.[45]

---

45. Dr. Courtney Bickel Lamberth, who kindly read this chapter and helped me to clarify a central point in Kant's philosophy, asked the question that will likely arise for many readers: What "new avenues for theological work" does the concept "new covenant of life" open? It is a question that I cannot address here but one that surely will accompany me as I continue to work on the intriguing topic of biblical tradition and political process. I also want to express my gratitude to Prof. Michael Welker of the Universität Heidelberg for pressing me to clarify one major facet of Isaiah's message, namely, how his experience of the Holy One differed from the phenomenon described by Rudolph Otto in his book, *Idea of the Holy*. A final acknowledgement of indebtedness I owe to my colleague, Ronald F. Thiemann, who, both through his writings and in personal conversations, has deepened my understanding of the issues at stake in the debate between communitarians, pragmatists and liberals. Though not eliminating my own sense of inadequacy to address the complex issues raised at the point of intersection between religion and politics, the willingness of these theologians to engage in conversation with a biblical scholar is a source of stimulation and encouragement.

4 *Jesus Christ, Savior and the Human Condition: The Biblical Background*

In the preceding chapters we have seen abundant evidence that religion, in the past as in the present, is capable of great good and dreadful harm. And people of faith are denied the comfort of pointing fingers solely at the atrocities perpetrated by other religious communities, for the history of no religion is free from the dark moments of the infliction of suffering on those who differ and collaboration with unjust leaders.

The task of explanation is relatively simple for atheistic philosophers like Arthur Schopenhauaer (1788–1860) and Ludwig Feuerbach (1804–1872) for whom religions are purely human constructs, and as such naturally reflective of the mixture of good and evil characteristic of the human race in general. Matters are more complicated for those who confess that at the heart of authentic religion lies the self-disclosure of a Being unblemished by the flaws of human nature. But even for such, the challenge takes different shapes depending on the understanding of that self-disclosure. For those subscribing to the notion of biblical inerrancy, the answer comes in the form of deriving from a literal reading of the Bible the nature and will of the God revealed therein. On the other hand, for these who believe that God's self-disclosure was mediated by the generations of believing communities that encountered God in the events of their history and gave testimony to God's presence in the writings that now constitute the Bible, another element is added, namely, attention to the role of finite human understanding both in the original writings and in the subsequent, long history of interpretation.

The vastly different portraits of God and God's will that one finds both historically and in the present day draw attention to the subjective element that is present in every endeavor to grasp the meaning of Scripture. It underlines the importance of careful attention to the phenomenon of interpretation, not the least because of the serious implications that a particular grasp of biblical truth has for life in a complex world. To give one example, one can consider the vastly different conclusions that emerge for foreign policy on the basis of two understandings of God's relation to the role of the United States in world events, on the one hand, a God who has chosen the U.S. to determine the course of events and the power relations between contending nations in the Middle East, and on the other hand, a God holding no favorites, presiding as the judge over the powerful and the weak, and willing equality and justice for all nations.

It is to the urgent and politically charged task of sorting through the rival images of God, and concomitantly, of the understanding of the human condition stemming from those images, that we turn in this chapter. We shall seek to describe popular construals of God and of the human condition and then measure them against the nature of God and the human found in the Bible. We shall do so by parsing the *topos*, "Jesus Christ Savior and the Human Condition."[1] But first a few introductory thoughts.

A serious problem that communities of faith must revisit constantly is that humans tend to whittle their gods down to a size that suits their own purposes with scant attention to the unco-opted and universal scope of the God described by Israel's prophets. This issue takes on serious political dimensions when such whittling is found among religious leaders lobbying for domestic programs that contradict biblical notions of even-handed justice and compassion for the poor and promoting foreign policies dedicated to national self-interest at the expense of the security and prosperity of other nations.

While it may seem like an oxymoron to call a god who sponsors the programs of the world's greatest economic and military super-power a whittled down deity, we propose in this chapter to expose to critique based on biblical prophetic tradition the kind of

1. This *topos* is taken from the theme of a study sponsored by the Center for Theological Inquiry of Princeton, NJ, in the academic year 2003–04.

nationalistic religious patriotism that has plagued U.S. foreign policy from its early years and has loomed ever larger as the nation grew to super-power status. Our investigation will yield the stark fact that no matter how grandiose the portrait of a god subservient to nationalistic self-interest may be, such a god is a pitiable mockery of true divinity. For example, when Second Isaiah witnessed the parading of Marduk and Nebo around the walls of Babylon, he ridiculed those who wearied the beasts of burden carrying cumbersome idols that were empty of power and whose sole significance resided in their being an affront to the one true God and a snare for those who fell down to worship them. The essence of the prophetic message is that nationalistic religion categorically is idolatrous, inasmuch as it blasphemes the one God alone worthy of honor, the God in whose eyes no nation could claim special privilege, the God who viewed every human, regardless of nationality or status, as equal, the God who judged nations not on their economic or cultural accomplishments, but alone on the basis of the divine standard of protection of the poor, even-handed administration of justice, and policies that fostered peace with other nations.

Those who cultivate an image of a patron deity that is subservient to the objectives of a given nation are ignorant of the awesome Creator and Ruler of the universe who is the God encountered in Scripture. This, of course, is a serious accusation, one that inevitably stirs up controversy. But to remain silent for the sake of patriotic solidarity or inner-Christian harmony is not an option commended by the Bible or by the lessons of church history.

Many of the theological battles over the centuries have stemmed from divergent understandings of Scripture. The early church fathers did not flee from battle when the unity of Scripture was threatened by Marcion's differentiating the creator God of the Old Testament from the savior God of the New Testament. Martin Luther stirred up a storm by insisting that the Bible be made available to ordinary people in their vernacular language. Sadly, he in turn reintroduced a serious theological problem by drawing an artificially sharp contrast between Old Testament Law and New Testament Gospel. While John Calvin proved to be more judicious in constructing a covenantal theology that preserved the integrity of both Testaments, sixteenth-century controversies over the Bible raged on, with the Roman Catholic Church taking the initiative in the Council of Trent. Asserting that the religious wars that plagued Europe were the inevitable result of each believer becoming his or her own interpreter of the Bible, the theologians who gathered at that Council reasserted the importance of the authoritative teaching function of the Church, that is, the Magisterium.

A significant turn in the Protestant-Catholic conflict came in the mid-seventeenth century, when the Calvinist theologian Francis Turretin defended the Protestant view of Scripture by claiming that the authority of the Magisterium was unnecessary, since the Bible was the sole authority needed, the truthfulness of which was safeguarded by its being the *inerrant* word of God. Turretin's position was developed into a high view of biblical inspiration in the U.S. by the so-called Princeton theologians (Charles Hodge, B. B. Warfield, and John Gresham Machen), whose efforts to restore conservative Calvinism as a bulwark against modernism led to their departure from Princeton and the founding of Westminster Theological Seminary in Philadelphia. To their efforts can be traced the spread of an ultraconservative view of biblical authority in the U.S. that built upon the concept of biblical inerrancy. Subsequently, what has come to be called Fundamentalism has become a major force in the U.S., especially as it ended a period of isolation from the mainstream and modulated into a determined political movement exercising considerable influence on national elections, judicial appointments, and local politics.

The adoption of the concept of inerrancy by a growing number of theological faculties had long-lasting effects on the controversies revolving around biblical hermeneutics. Today, inerrancy and the related concept of infallibility define the hermeneutic that prevails among Fundamentalist groups such as the Religious Right, the Moral Majority, and the Christian Coalition. Unfortunately, a hermeneutic based on inerrancy, rather than safeguarding the word of God in the Bible, abets what we have called the whittling down of God to a size suiting the interpreter. Concomitantly, it involves a whittling down of the Bible into a phenomenon that poignantly has been labeled "bibliolatry." The prophetic message excoriating human exploitation of the poor, the accumulation of wealth by the rich, and the distortion of universal divine justice into defense of one nation's imperialism is degraded into slogans like, "The Bible says it, I believe it, and that settles it." Though ostensibly describing a complete obedience to God's word, such slogans disguise the fact that every act of biblical interpretation involves the presuppositions of the interpreter. Self-deception and absolutism inevitably follow.

What claims to be a purely objective submission to divine will is, in reality, the identification of God's word with a human extrapolation that is removed from the benefit of self-criticism and discernment chastened by the scrutiny of others. The fundamental error lying at the heart of such absolutism is that it contradicts the central Christian truth expressed in the Incarnation—that God chooses to be present to humans in the only manner in which humans are capable of grasping that which utterly transcends their being and understanding, namely, through the mediating agency of things human. That is to say, God comes to humans in the fully human Jesus Christ and in the human words that comprise the Bible. This is not a lower view of biblical authority in comparison to the Fundamentalist view. Indeed, by testifying to the miracle that God reaches down to humans by participating in their world within their structures of thought and being, Christians preserve the central message of the Gospel.

In Scripture, we encounter God's incarnate presence in the Son and in the Word, even as in the Eucharist we encounter Christ in bread and wine. In the presence of God thus revealed, we are not handed a recipe book that provides answers such as, "Mr. President, you shall go to war," or "Ms. State School Board member, you shall order the teaching of Creationism in all schools." Decisions, of course, will have to be made by those elected to represent the people; and if they are Christians, their decisions will be influenced and tested by their worship, prayer and study of Scripture within the context of their faith community. Moreover, they will recognize that over the course of biblical history, God disclosed his will to his people through the law and the prophets, and on that scriptural basis succeeding generations of believers have engaged in ongoing interpretation leading to the formulation of beliefs and moral principles central to the Christian faith. Nevertheless, thorough understanding of the classics of the faith will not obscure but heighten awareness of the ambiguities that are intrinsic to human existence and the limited understanding that is a part of human nature will commend a diligent approach to biblical study characterized by humility, openness to the witness of God's interpreting community both past and present, and care not to succumb to the temptation of carelessly identifying personal or partisan or nationalistic interests with God's will.

Within the confines of the present chapter, it will not be possible to examine all facets of a faithful hermeneutic. That is the reason we have chosen to delimit our examination of the public witness of the Christian church by focusing on each of the terms in the *topos*: *Jesus Christ, Savior and the Human Condition.*

In looking first to *popular* spirituality, we shall find scant attention to the living God of Scripture directing words of censure through the prophets to corrupt political and business leaders, words of admonition to judges, and words of empowerment to the poor and the oppressed. All too frequently we shall encounter an icon smiling on those living in comfort and assuring them that their prosperity is a sign of the favor they enjoy in the eyes of their god. Like the dreamy New Age music that dulls the senses into lethargy, we find a designer god cut down to a size that makes his clients feel loved and comforted, a god supportive of personal desires, a god coming to earth to provide prosperity for the individual believer, rather than to disturb those living in luxury with imperatives relating to world hunger, pandemics, and international conflict. This is a god adapted to a society that is individualistic, consumer-driven, and complacent toward the wider world, the world of teeming masses of the poor and starving, the world of nature suffering from the exploitation of a wasteful society.

How contemporary world spirituality got mired down in such a narrow view of reality is a long and complicated story, but the New Testament scholar Krister Stendahl, in an important essay first published in 1963, argued that early signs of this development can be glimpsed in a distorted reinterpretation of the Apostle Paul driven by what he called "the introspective conscience of the West."[2] The cosmic breadth of the biblical salvation drama, and specifically the concept of justification as depicted in Romans, is downsized in this reinterpretation to fit into the brooding anxiety of the individual soul. The Enlightenment placed this soul at the center of the universe, and Kierkegaard and Nietzsche, each in his own way, further narrowed human consciousness in the direction of emotivism. What effect has the tunnel-vision of introspective philosophy had on the popular understanding of the meaning and significance of *Jesus Christ, Savior and the Human Condition*? After answering that question, we shall ask how the popular understanding compares to one shaped by the testimony of the Bible.

JESUS CHRIST

We begin with "Jesus Christ," which for many moderns conforms to the onomastic pattern NN, as in John Hancock, that is, given name followed by surname. This would imply that if you did not have a close relationship with this God, you would introduce him formally as "Mr. Christ." But the sentimental believer we are describing has more than a formal relationship with God's son. In fact, it can be described as an intimate relative, expressed in emotional outpourings in worship and in romantic lyrics descriptive of two lovers oblivious of anyone else in the whole world: "He walks with me, and he talks with me, and He tells me I am His own: And the joy we share as we tarry there, *None other* has ever known" (italics added). The dread sense of awe traditionally associated with encounter with the Holy One is replaced with the blissful warmth of an indulgent lover.

Description and critique of the individualist/emotivist understanding of Jesus Christ would be easier if it could be objectified and sealed off from personal experience. In my case, that is impossible because I grew up in the midst of such piety, which means I cannot simply condemn it dispassionately and categorically; I must strive to understand it as the conscientious belief of good people

2. Stendahl, "The Apostle Paul and the Introspective Conscience of the West."

seeking to be true to the Christian faith. I can express my love and respect for them, however, not by cutting myself from dialogue out of a disdainful sense of superiority (a common reaction to the "folks back home" by many intellectual Christians), but by expressing my love and respect in sharing my reasons for believing that such an understanding of God is narrower than the understanding developed in Scripture and my sense that it is the product not of classical Christianity but of "the introspective conscience of the West." Through genuine dialogue Christians of all denominations can join in the study and self-searching that can permit the Alpha and Omega to reclaim the space now occupied in our hearts by the whittled down, domesticated Jesus walking with us in the garden alone.

Now I venture to offer an example of how close to home this matter is for me. When my wife Cynthia and I embarked upon our teaching careers, our home was a big Victorian house that we shared with two other couples as a small commune. Living adjacent to us on the second floor was my nephew and his wife, both of them adhering to a more conservative expression of Christianity than their uncle and aunt. In fact, my nephew's wife was Charismatic and Fundamentalist. Christ was by her side to clarify her every decision, including the location of her first teaching assignment. Hence, she was able to announce to us that she was being led to teach in an inner-city school, one Cynthia and I recognized as belonging to a community whose school system presented serious disciplinary challenges. With a certainty sustained by following Christ's personally delivered directive that required no further inquiry or discernment, my niece began the school year. For a time, an increasingly difficult classroom situation was addressed by her preparing for the day by speaking in tongues behind the steering wheel on her lengthy daily commute. Before long, however, matters seemed to decline, finally spiraling out of control. One morning at breakfast, the rather sullen mood to which we had grown accustomed was replaced by a cheery announcement that Jesus had directed her to another job in a private Christian academy located in an affluent suburb.

The question arises as to the source of divine directives in such situations. Is God in Christ being experienced as the Sovereign

Ruler to whose will, though grasped imperfectly, we submit, or does God's Son function as the enabling agent substantiating our own perceptions and desires, whether they are conscientious (as were my niece's) or base. If Jesus in the above example functions as alter ego, is the God of the Bible not in danger of being whittled down to an image resembling the idols fashioned by human hands attacked by Isaiah and Jeremiah? The question cannot be raised with a self-righteous attitude, inasmuch as we are all idol-builders in our own ways and in specific areas of our own human existence, with the major difference being that some idols will be imbued with liberal qualities, others with more conservative ones. I suggest that we dare raise such questions only if we are receptive to the same honest questioning when directed to us by others. How else can we begin to loosen the shackles of an exploitative use of religion to prepare the way for faithful discipleship?

We turn to the second title in the topos we are examining. In popular religion, the epithet "Savior" is perceived as pointing to Jesus' primary function of saving the individual Christian from the adversities of this evil age. The connotation is also expressed in the fuller epithet, "my personal Lord and Savior." The God of the Bible, to be sure, is portrayed as attentive to the needs of every individual, but this does not diminish God s concern for the creation in its vastness and complexity. Once again, we are dealing with the reduction of the biblical God to a size suitable for an individualist, introspective conscience.

Many televangelists, for example, present a Savior available at a moment's notice to heal everything from cancer to mental illness. I was once invited by a postal solicitation to contribute to a ministry headquartered in Tulsa, Oklahoma, a contribution that guaranteed to activate the healing properties of a piece of cloth that accompanied the letter. The pitch of that Crusade, whose principal symbol interestingly was not the cross but a cornucopia, was that generosity to the Osborn ministry would be rewarded by manifold blessings, including miraculous health and wealth.[3] Let us now consider two

---

3. A similar ministry thriving on the heady days on Wall Street preceding the recession of 2008–2009 was described in a *New York Times* article by Michael Luo, "Preaching a Gospel of Wealth in a Glittery Market."

forms that savior-as-personal-deliverer takes in popular spirituality, namely, personalism and apocalypticism.

Personalism flourishes in affinity groups characterized by sentimentalism and a preoccupation with signs of election and divine favor. Outreach beyond this inner circle is usually motivated by saving souls rather than addressing systemic inequality, hunger, international conflict, and epidemic disease. The underlying assumption is that the world is hopelessly fallen to sin and, in effect, is on the path to self-destruction, necessitating a Savior to deliver the chosen few from the impending doom. Closely associated is the view that the impoverished and diseased are reaping the fruits of their own dereliction. Among the affluent, personalism flourishes in gated communities that are a travesty of the Apostle Paul's "body of Christ," inasmuch as they, like a country club, are self-selecting. Indeed, Paul's stinging words in 1 Corinthians 11:17–22 still apply to churches in which Sunday morning worship finds Christians divided along the social, racial, and economic lines that tear apart the fabric of society and contradict the biblical ideal of the family of all God's children. To paraphrase Paul, if we celebrate the Lord's Supper and we are divided with one group eating and drinking (literally "becoming drunk!") and the other going hungry, we show contempt for the Body of Christ. We are like those exhibiting sham piety in Isaiah 1, whom God repudiates because the hands they raise in prayer are hands stained with the blood of the poor whom they have exploited and oppressed.

Another form that self-indulgent personalist spirituality takes is apocalypticism. It is a mode of religious comfort and hope offered by those construing their personal wealth as evidence of divine favor to those who have responded positively to their missionary appeal, but whose lives give no evidence of their sharing in the benefits of the good life on earth enjoyed by their patrons. The form of "gospel" designed for them insists that they should not be concerned about their deprivation in this world, since experiences like ill health without the benefit of health insurance, substandard housing, and lack of educational opportunities for their children all pale in comparison to the "make-up" rewards awaiting them beyond the grave.

In the case of both forms of personalist piety, biblical truths are present, but present in a distorted form and cut off from broader aspects of the biblical notion of salvation. The urgent call for social justice and inclusive human care found in the message of the Hebrew prophets and Jesus Christ is eclipsed by a preoccupation with personal assurances of divine favor and blessing. All too easily, this whittled-down version of Christianity nurtures a self-righteous dismissal of the poor as lazy, the diseased as cursed, and the dispossessed as reaping the fruits of the mismanagement of their own lives.

The comparison of the personalist understanding of Savior with the Savior who directed the lives of the martyrs and saints of the church is incriminating. Saint Francis of Assisi draws our attention to the God of the Bible whose loving care extended to all people, rich and poor, and to all creatures, great and small. Mother Teresa stands as an inspiring example of God's love embracing those deemed untouchable by the wider society. Sister Christine Tan, a woman born into privileged circumstances and benefiting from excellent education, gave up wealth and comfort to work with the poor of Manila. In the lives of these disciples, who chose to walk in the path of a Savior who explained that it was not the well who need a physician but the sick, we regain a true sense of the majesty of God, even as we are reminded of the pathetic nature of the idols we create to minister to our own petty needs and desires.

Complicating the matter is that those who fashion their own gods to fit their particular agendas frequently construct as a defense against criticism the armor of absolutism. In condemning the homosexual, the Muslim, the alcoholic, they claim simply to be applying the laws and truths of Scripture. That their aggressive defense rests on faulty theology is suggested by contrast with the posture of those who embody the compassion of Christ, those who devote their primary energy not to attacking the godless but in extending God's mercy and justice to those deemed by others as least deserving, those free of attempts to impose their understanding of biblical norms on fellow citizens by force, leaving to God the final judgment and thereby being free to live generously and mercifully in Christ's name. When it comes to their personal salvation, they express little anxiety, since their Savior is the Savior of the entire universe, one fully capable of caring for the obedient—albeit sinful and repentant—servant.

Having examined the manner in which humans in the contemporary world tend to reduce God to a size and to functions associated in the Bible with idols, we now direct our attention to the way in which the meaning of "Jesus Christ, Savior and the Human Condition" is transformed when understood in light of the Bible in its entirety. We begin with the Apostle Paul's historical observation in Romans 9:5: "From the Israelites comes the Christ." It was clear to Paul that God had been preparing for the coming of the Messiah for a long, long time before the birth of a baby in a Bethlehem stable. It is this truth that was preserved by classical Christianity in the doctrine of the Trinity: The nativity of Christ was not one moment in time, but involved preparation from the foundation of the earth and reflected God's unending commitment to his creation. The angel who announced Christ's birth got it right, "to you is born this day in the City of David a Savior who is the Messiah, the Lord" (Luke 2:11).

Just two chapters later in Luke's Gospel, we receive a vivid picture of the nature of this Messiah (i.e., Christ) Savior. In Nazareth on Shabbat, he is given the scroll of the prophet Isaiah to read in the synagogue. The lection is Isaiah 61:1–3, which he interprets as describing his own ministry: "bringing good news to the poor," "proclaiming release to the captives," "sight to the blind," "freedom for the oppressed," all signs of the long-awaited "year of the Lord's favor." Jesus announces that through his words and deeds, the Jubilee was entering into the fabric of human social existence with all of its God-intended healing effects.

Nothing captures the heart of Israelite communal ideals as succinctly as the Jubilee, which, as described in Leviticus, is the forty-ninth year in which all social and economic structures were to be returned to the state intended by God: debts were to be forgiven, slaves released, and each family that had lost its land through foreclosure restored to its inheritance. This introduction to Jesus' ministry, combined with the ongoing narrative of Jesus' healing, feeding, and sustaining those in need, sets the stage for a reinterpretation of Jesus Christ, Savior and the human condition that breaks asunder the narrow picture of Jesus provided by popular introspective religion.

Replacing the image of a genie god catering to the wishes of individuals craving for God's special favor is the extravagantly generous God inspiring Millard and Linda Fuller to found Habitat for Humanity through initial funding from their own wealth skillfully leveraged by means of the organization of a large cadre of volunteers and resulting in affordable housing for families who otherwise were unable even to dream of home ownership, and the God of justice prompting the British economist Martin Dent and Chancellor of the Exchequer and later Prime Minister Gordon Brown to act on the biblical vision of a restored humanity through Jubilee 2000, a international program dedicated to removing the crippling weight of debt from the poorest nations of the world. Such contemporary examples invite the faithful to shed the bondage of introspective conscience and to enter the reform movement of the One proclaiming the year of Jubilee not just for the few but for the whole human family, indeed, for the entire cosmos.

In the case of Jesus of Nazareth, the bondage from which humans needed to be released was enforced by the ruthless might of the Roman Empire. The contemporary world has produced its counterparts in the form of multi-national corporations and competing nation-states utilizing the weapons of economic power and military might to control markets in commodities and manufactured goods and when necessary ignoring the plight of peasants and commoners or crushing their demands for a fair share of the wealth as obstacles to the free flow of vital natural resources and investment capital. Now as then, hunger, sickness, mental anguish, and violence are spawned by the perversion of justice and mercy feeding the insatiable appetites of the world's richest individuals, corporations and nations. And all too often, we as members of the church remain silent, or we are satisfied with contributions that amount to little more than the crumbs falling from the banquet tables of the rich to their dogs beneath. Though some will argue that such criticism of whittled-down gods is overly harsh, cynical, and above all unpatriotic, it comes closer to the spirit of the biblical prophets than the persisting mood that an earlier biblical scholar described as "The Strange Silence of the Bible in the Church."[4] Not silence but honest testimony is the necessary first step in exorcising the idols that abet human misery and making room for the living God who seeks the healing of all that is broken. In daring to take that step, let us move on in our reconsideration of the biblical meaning of Jesus Christ Savior and the human condition.

Jesus is a typical biblical name, conforming to the same onomastic pattern as the name my wife and I gave to our son Nathaniel in acknowledgment of our joy and gratitude for this most wondrous gift. Translated from Hebrew to English, Nathaniel means "gift of God." Jesus' parents, following ancient Jewish custom, named their son *Yešua'* (<*Yehošua'*), that is, "Yahweh is salvation." In this sentence name, the deity as subject is linked to the Hebrew verb *yš'*, which is used frequently in the Old Testament to describe God's deliverance of his people from their enslavement or adversity. In what may be the oldest poem in the Bible, Moses (originally Miriam!) invokes that same root on behalf of the people in celebrating Yahweh as "my salvation" (Exodus 15:2). In another ancient poem, the passive form of the verb forms a lovely epithet for Israel as the object of God's deliverance (Deuteronomy 33:29). Its literal translation is "a people saved by God." It thus becomes apparent that the name given to Jesus adumbrates the divine purpose to which he has been born, the purpose of saving God's people, and more broadly, humanity from bondage.

The biblical connotations of Christ are similarly rich. It is not a simple surname, but a title rich in meaning and significance. The Greek *christos* (χριστός) preserves the meaning of the Hebrew word it translates, namely מָשִׁיחַ (*mašîah*), literally "Anointed One." It designates one who has been divinely appointed, appointed by God to a specific office. Jesus comes into the world as savior, appointed, anointed to his office. It is not a casual designation. Jesus was prepared, and then anointed by the Father for his job. The passage mentioned earlier from Luke 4, in which Jesus cites Isaiah 61 as descriptive of his ministry, begins: "The Spirit of the Lord is upon

4. Smart, *The Strange Silence of the Bible in the Church*.

me, because He has anointed (*echrisen* <*mâšah*) me to bring good news to the poor, to release captives, to announce the chosen day of the Lord." The "chosen day," as noted above, refers to the Jubilee. Jesus the Christ, then, is Yeshua, the One anointed by God for a distinct mission, one that is broadly social in nature and revolutionary in relation to the prevailing economic structures that held normal people in poverty and subservience to the wealthy. While it is clear that the good news proclaimed by Jesus Christ included words of promise of salvation to the individual, it was not good news that stopped with the individual, but set in motion a redemptive drama that embraced the universe. As the Apostle Paul saw so clearly, Christians collectively constituted Christ's body in the world and became ambassadors actively participating in the healing of the universe (תִּקּוּן עוֹלָם, *tiqqûn 'olam*).

The Christ, to whose purpose the redeemed are called, is further described in our epithet as Savior. We have seen that the title Savior frequently is assimilated in popular religion to a construal of God as personal attendant to the wishes of the individual. The biblical depiction of the Savior erases a petty personalistic caricature and confronts the person of faith with the God whose saving agenda embraces all humans and all creation.

SAVIOR

In the ancient Greek Old Testament (the Septuagint) σωτήρ (*sōtēr*, "savior") translates various forms of the Hebrew root יָשַׁע (*yš'*), thereby designating God or one appointed by God as Deliverer or Savior of Israel from enemy threats. This word σωτήρ was widely applied in the New Testament to describe Jesus as the Savior of those suffering under the oppressive conditions of the Roman Empire, even as it was used to depict Christ's abiding presence as the faithful moved through the tribulations of a world viewed apocalyptically as approaching its final judgment.

The political ramifications of the title Savior come into view in light of the epithet commonly used by the Roman emperors to describe themselves within the imperial cult, namely "god and savior."

In the New Testament, this imperial epithet for Augustus is exposed as counterfeit and reclaimed by the only ruler worthy of the name Savior, the Messiah sent by God to introduce what the *Pax Romana* deceptively claimed to preserve, a universal and eternal reign of peace and justice. Thus, we see that it is not sufficient to limit our understanding of Jesus Christ to "my personal Savior," for in the New Testament he not only attends to individual needs, but challenges the hubris and apostasy of Caesar Augustus and inaugurates a counterforce that seeks to replace injustice and oppression with justice, mercy, and "peace on earth, goodwill to all humanity."

Professor Amy-Jill Levine, in a lecture delivered in Manila in 2004, drew attention to a neglected connotation of another New Testament title, namely Father.[5] Commonly, one reads that, in the Gospels, Father (Aramaic אַבָּא, *'abba'*) was an epithet echoing the intimacy of a child addressing her father, the equivalent of "daddy" in English vernacular. This popular understanding overlooks an important political dimension, for once again, the Roman Caesars were addressed as "Father." In other words, Jesus reclaims the title that had been "hijacked" by impostors and restores it as an important signifier of the special relationship uniting the true Father and his Son in their task of restoring lasting structures of compassionate justice. Thus, if Father is restricted to a meaning conveying a cozy daddy-child relationship, the universal power of the Heavenly Father is seriously truncated.[6]

An important lesson is thus learned from the example of the early Christians as they lived under the Roman imperium, whether as disenfranchised commoners like the vast majority of believers or as full citizens like the Apostle Paul. We exchange our Christian faith for a pagan idolatry if we uncritically pledge our allegiance to nation or political party, for the Christian reserves ultimate loyalty for one regime alone, God's reign. True patriotism must not be confused with nationalistic ideology, since we contribute most genuinely to the strength and stability of our own nation when we insist that it measure up to the divine standards of impartial universal justice.

5. Levine, "Jesus and Judaism: Why the Connection Still Matters," 64–65.
6. See Barr "Abba Isn't Daddy."

Paul states this biblical truth poignantly in Philippians 3:20: "But our citizenship is in heaven, and it is from there that we are expecting a Savior (σωτήρ), the Lord Jesus Christ." Jesus Christ Savior, when read within its New Testament context of Roman rule and understood against the background of Old Testament salvation history, presents more than a "bailiff" standing at the beck and call of the individual. To be sure, in the breaking of the bread, there is revealed to us as to the Apostles a God present to us in our personal need. But beyond the sphere of our personal need is revealed to us the Savior of the world asking us, "Is your nation forsaking me by not using the full extent of its political and economic influence to save women and children in Darfur who have been displaced by war and are now suffering the ravages of malnutrition? Has your affluence blinded yourselves to the fact that you insist on a lifestyle that is both further impoverishing the poor and degrading the entire creation?" We each have our own ways of denying that the God we worship is the universal Savior actively calling us to participate in healing all that is broken by doing justice, loving kindness, and walking humbly with our God in all aspects of our lives. We repent of our denial of God's reign when we confess that our citizenship is in heaven and then order all of our affairs, personal and public, in harmony with the will of the heavenly Father, including those affairs that have to do with the everyday and the mundane.

There are moments in the life of the church that elicit a response clearly defining the ethical mandate of the Gospel. The Barman Declaration denouncing the nationalistic idolatry of Nazism is one example. The American Roman Catholic bishops' letter on economic justice is another.[7] With prophetic audacity, that modern epistle to the churches declared that the God of the Bible calls for a "preferential option for the poor." Such incisive stands taken against evil and on behalf of justice prove that the practice of "biblical politics" *is* possible in the modern world. And a starting point for any community devoted to human dignity and equality is identification with the biblical pageant. For even a cursory survey of Scripture demonstrates that the God of Israel and Messiah Jesus placed no agenda

7. *Economic Justice for All.*

higher than caring for the poor.[8] In fact, the biblical drama begins with a God who defeats the rival slave-holding "god" Pharaoh on behalf of those in bondage. The prophets continued that battle in risking their lives to defend the rights of the neglected poor against powerful native kings and nobility. And in the gospels Jesus is found most frequently in the company of the poor, and he promises that they will be the blessed inheritors of the Kingdom of peace and justice that the Father has sent him to restore.

The most tempting contemporary defense against advocating for incisive action against exploitation, deprivation, disease and neo-colonialist economic policies is the claim that in contrast to the situation of the Jews living under Roman occupation or the Germans living under the iron fist of the Nazis, our times are relatively peaceful, calling for moderate policies dedicated to gradual change. One version of this approach has come to be identified as "trickle down economics." The equivalent biblical metaphor would be the crumbs falling to the hungry dogs under the table. But this approach seems to rest upon the twin deceptions of misrepresenting the degree of injustice that exists in most of the world today and ignoring the paradigm of political response to injustice that is provided unequivocally by the Bible, regardless of whether one focuses on the Hebrew prophets or Jesus of Nazareth. The church that takes the comfortable approach of supporting the "normalcy" argument is a pandering church, exposing itself to the heavenly Judge's condemnation of the church of Laodicea, known for works that were "lukewarm, and neither cold nor hot" (Revelation 3:16).

THE HUMAN CONDITION

We now take the next step in our discussion to consider the final element in our *topos*, the human condition. We do this on the assumption, clearly set forth by Karl Barth, that anthropology is un-

8. Jim Wallis (an Evangelical Christian social progressive) is tireless in pointing out to fellow Evangelicals that the Bible's ubiquitous advocacy for the poor, in contrast to its virtual silence on issues of homosexuality and abortion, should be raised to top-priority status by political activists of the Religious Right.

derstood aright by the Christian only if interpreted through the lens of Christology, and with the hope that we have presented with a reasonable degree of accuracy the biblical understanding of Jesus Christ Savior.

What then is the biblical understanding of the human condition? The Old Testament contains a consistent picture of the human condition, a picture inherited and developed further in the writings of the New Testament, as well in the works of the church's leading theologians like St. Augustine, Thomas Aquinas, and Martin Luther. It is not the anthropology popularized in the lyrics of *Jesus Christ Superstar*, "Everything's alright, yes, everything's fine," for it reflects a more sober view of the world. But neither is it a view leading to futility, for an intrinsic part of the biblical confession is that creation was not intended by God to engulf humans in sin and travail forever, but to be redeemed and restored to its original integrity. Biblical anthropology therefore can be characterized as a dialectical anthropology. This is seen already in Genesis 1:31: God culminates his creative activity by creating the human, and as in the case of everything else God had created, "God saw everything he had made and indeed it was good." God was pleased that He had created a good thing when he created humans. In Psalm 8:5, King David marvels at God's handiwork: "You have made him little less than divine and adorned him with glory and majesty."

Over against this view of the goodness of humanity is the dialectical turn that appears already in Genesis 6:5[9] and is reinforced repeatedly in the prophetic writings. Jeremiah, for example, despairs over a human seemingly incorrigible in the ways of wickedness, and he recognizes the destruction of Judah by the Babylonian armies as the inevitable consequence. He searches for an explanation and finally concludes, "The heart is devious above all else; it is perverse—who can understand it?" (Jeremiah 17:9). For the one hoping to find a rosier picture in the New Testament, Romans 7:18 must come as a great disappointment: "For I know that nothing good dwells in me, that is in the flesh. I can will what is right but I cannot do it."

9. "The LORD saw that the wickedness of humankind was great upon the earth, and that every inclination of the thoughts of their hearts was only evil continually."

Paul therefore sharpens the dialectic, and leaves us with what, on the surface, appears to be a contradiction, the human as little less than divine, and devious above all else. One could adopt the solution proposed by the Gnostics: The embodied human is imprisoned in corruption with hope for salvation only by finding a Redeemer to snatch the soul from the body and return it to the pure realm of Spirit. Christianity denounced that simple solution, insisting instead on recognizing God's saving activity within the dialectic of the human condition.

In Romans 8:20, the Apostle succinctly formulated the dialectic at the heart of the human condition by claiming God "subjected it to futility, in hope." According to Paul's interpretation, the suffering that was so much a part of both human and non-human creation was not viewed naturalistically, but theologically as judgment occurring with the context of a covenantal relationship. What is truly remarkable is that, the dark assessment of unaided human potential notwithstanding, judgment in the last analysis is viewed not negatively but as a stage in God's redemptive activity, that is, "in hope." This means that if humans are in trouble, which is hard to deny, it is because of God's involvement in human history, an involvement whose final purpose is the restoration of human and natural creation to the beauty and harmony the Hebrew Bible calls *shalom*. The presence of judgment, therefore, is evidence that God, through all of the assaults on his will, has managed to uphold a moral universe in which wrongdoing brings consequences that cry out for incisive corrective action like Abel's blood from the saturated ground.

The popular response to the unflinching realism of biblical anthropology is parallel to its response to the biblical view of Jesus Christ Savior, namely, to whittle it down to a simple, benign picture. What we want to preserve is an image of ourselves that is not as negative as parts of the Bible seem to suggest. Courageously, the Apostle Paul located the confluence of the world's abhorrence to the biblical portrayal of the suffering incarnate God and its denial of the fallen human condition at a single point in history, the "scandal" of the cross (1 Corinthians 1:22–24). Yet the biblical truth about the human plight and God's radical response to it cannot be hidden from view, for wherever the church has been faithful in its testimony, it has presented that truth, whether in the crucifix above the altar of a Gothic cathedral, in Luther's description of the theology of the cross, or in a contemporary cinematic portrait of the *via dolorosa*.[10] The ubiquity of the motif does not diminish the reflexive tendency of humans to shun the stark truth lying at the center of Scripture. In my experience within casual social settings, once I have been identified as an "Old Testament scholar," the most common (and passionate) objection raised to the God of the Bible is his bellicose response to his enemies—enemies, note well—such as wealthy oppressors of the poor, kings claiming divine prerogatives, religious leaders promoting self-interest through earthly collusion with influential potentates, etc. The major premise that must inform one's understanding of divine judgment in the Bible is therefore the following: The biblical picture of the human condition is predicated on a remarkably consistent view of the universe as a moral sphere, that is, a view according to which violation of basic ethical principles brings consequences. The church must not capitulate to sentimental popular construals of God as indulgent Father, of Jesus as personal Benefactor, and of wealth as proof of divine favor.

To affirm that the universe portrayed by the Bible is moral is not to imply that that portrait is static. Presented as a part of the testimony of the faith community, it reflects growth in understanding, or to state the same point theologically, an awareness that God's revelation is ongoing throughout the chapters of biblical history. A magisterial presentation of that moral universe is found in Deuteronomy, as summarized by these verses: "I call heaven and earth to witness against you today that I have set before you life and death, blessings and curses. Choose life so that you and your descendants may live, loving the LORD your God, obeying him and holding fast to him" (Deuteronomy 30:19–20). Naturally, it is God's will that the human community choose the way of obedience and blessing. When the path of disobedience and self-assertion is chosen, if God were to respond with indifference, the result would be an amoral universe, one incapable of sustaining any semblance of or-

10. Mel Gibson's portrait of Christ in *The Passion of the Christ* serves as an example here, regardless of one's assessment of the alleged anti-Semitic elements in his film.

der, whether in the realm of personal relations, social institutions, or international affairs. To be sure, this Deuteronomic formulation also could be debased, as it frequently is today when riches on this earth are promised as the reward for conformity to a particular preacher's message. It is significant that the Book of Job was preserved as a part of Scripture, for it warns against every mechanical interpretation of divine retribution. Confidence in the moral order of life and assurance of God's faithfulness involves a perspective vastly transcending the narrow orbit of personal existence. As we shall see in discussing Romans 8, when grasped aright, it is an understanding stretched to encompass the entire cosmos.

Before turning to the cosmic drama of redemption in the Bible, however, it is necessary to grasp a fuller picture of the way the human condition is presented in the Old Testament. The prophet Hosea builds upon the theology of Deuteronomy. As he surveys his nation, he witnesses a rapid moral decline, with wealthy entrepreneurs impoverishing the poor, judges trampling over the rights of the commoner and political leaders plunging the nation deeper and deeper into futile international conflicts. From his viewpoint, more is at stake than misguided human strategies; he recognizes that the covenant that alone can establish Israel's security has been broken. He sees a fracturing of the moral core of the universe. He sees a God filled with compassion and sadness witnessing humans stubbornly determined to bring about their own ruin. And God's heart yearns for these people, much as Jesus cried for the children of Jerusalem (Hosea 11:8; Matthew 23:37 // Luke 13:34). In spite of that profound love, Hosea realizes that God cannot allow their crimes to go unpunished. He sees that if God does not judge a wayward nation, then on the authority of the Creator, the universe will be declared amoral, a chaotic sphere where anything goes, where righteousness and wickedness are undifferentiated, where tender kindness and cruelty are on a par. In three verses (4:1–3), Hosea depicts the rapid sequence that leads from human sin to cosmic disintegration. First, God brings an indictment against the people that points to the rupture of its covenant relationship: "There is no faithfulness or loyalty, and no knowledge of God in the land" (v. 1). Once the nucleus is rotten, the outbreak of every moral sickness is inevitable, which means that the social structure safeguarded by the Ten Commandments collapses: "Swearing, lying, and murder, and stealing and adultery break out; bloodshed follows bloodshed" (v. 2). But the devastation is not limited to the human realm, the physical landscape is engulfed as well: "Therefore the land mourns, and all who live in it languish; together with the wild animals and the birds of the air, even the fish of the sea are perishing" (v. 3).

A century after the Northern Kingdom, unmoved by Hosea's warning, was wiped off the map by Assyria, Jeremiah agonized as he witnessed the Southern Kingdom of Judah following the same path to ruin: "They are skilled in doing evil, but do not know how to do good" (Jeremiah 4:22). And like his predecessor Hosea, he too shuddered at the thought of consequences that would cast not just his nation but the world back into primordial chaos: "I look to the earth and lo, it was waste and void; and to the heavens, and they had no light" (Jeremiah 4:23). "Waste and void"—or in Hebrew, תהו ובהו (*tohû wabohû*)—is the formlessness that preexisted God's creative work in Genesis 1. Jeremiah could have employed no stronger image to state the dire seriousness of a human act that threatened to undo the divine act of creation. Nothing less than the divinely created beauty of the universe was placed in jeopardy by the dereliction of humans.

In Isaiah, we again see a prophet surveying nation and world, and experiencing the shock of an entire creation collapsing under the defilement of its human inhabitants:

> The earth dries up and withers,
>> the world languishes and withers;
>> the heavens languish together with the earth.
> The earth lies polluted
>> under its inhabitants;
> for they have transgressed laws,
>> violated the statutes,
>> broken the everlasting covenant.
> Therefore a curse devours the earth,
>> and its inhabitants suffer for their guilt. (Isaiah 24:4–6a)

Thus far, then, we have surveyed the dark side of the biblical account of the human condition, in Paul's words, a world "subjected to futility." But what of the other side of the dialectic constituting the anthropology of Scripture? Did not Paul write, "subjected to futility, *in hope?*"

For many conscientious, moral people, grounds for hope are more difficult to recognize than reasons for despair. And have we not cautioned earlier in this chapter against a facile understanding of salvation that denies the tragedy that engulfs the lives of so many of the earth's inhabitants? Did not Jeremiah excoriate against false prophets who announced "peace, peace, where there is no peace?" Do we need to look far even in our own society and world to see the futility? Over and over again I have heard, in the U.S. as well as in South Africa, the Philippines and India, a common lament among reformers on the edge of despair: "For thirty years the pattern continues. Corruption is rampant, parties campaign on promises to clean up the mess, to direct revenues back to those who have elected them in the form of social services, to prosecute politicians involved in payola from gambling organizations. We elect a new set of officials, taking them at their word, and what happens, they engage in the same corrupt practices as their predecessors." And despair over "the system" can lead to voter apathy. Why work for any political party when they are all corrupt? Futility, therefore, is not just an ancient phenomenon; it is rife within much of the world today. What can we say in defense of hope?

If it were not for a Reality transcending human agency, Christians would have every reason to join the disenfranchised cynics and anarchists and ex-reformers burned out by disappointment leading to despair. But in the biblical narrative, they find a story guided by a defiance vis-à-vis all that assails compassion and justice, for from the beginning, God destined humans for life in fellowship with the Creator and shared with them the divine image, enabling them to enjoy each other's communion in diverse vocations, as helpmates, leaders, followers, prophets, priests and judges, together constituting a community of civil-minded participants, each adding to the beauty of the social and natural world motivated by the vision of participating in a new birth.

Undeniably, that community over the ages and down to the present struggles against daunting obstacles, due to the obduracy of humans. But God does not abandon the faithful in their struggle, but provides prophets and preachers to remind them of their intended destiny. These prophets and preachers do not offer blithe solutions. They participate too profoundly in the suffering of their people to "treat the wound of my people carelessly" (Jeremiah 6:14). A profound sadness gripped the soul of Jeremiah as he viewed his nation. Aware of the care with which God nurtured a people for fellowship and shalom, he witnessed a nation contradicting its origins in divine mercy (Jeremiah 2:1–13). Repeatedly, he utilized his favorite verb, שוב (*šub*, "turn, return"), in appealing to their hearts: "if you return, Israel, to the Lord, if you return to me ..." (Jeremiah 4:1–3). The passionate nature of the appeal, re-enforced by repetition of the verb, conveys the seriousness of the call. The decision calls for more than a casual response, for it entails a reorientation of the whole being on the most profound level, a transformation of the corrupt, perverse human heart to the purity to will one thing, God's will. The noun corresponding to the verb שוב is תשובה (*tešubah*), which is translated into New Testament Greek as μετανοία (*metanoia*)—literally, turning around, or in theological terms, confession, repentance, and a new way of life, indeed, the Apostle Paul insists, a "new being"! In this audacious claim, Paul was simply drawing on the teaching of his ancestral faith. Christian and Jewish scriptures find one of their many moments of unified witness in declaring that opting for God's way, rather than the way of the world, involves a complete "overhaul." Jeremiah applies the metaphor of a new covenant, that is, not a change in God's eternal laws (תורה, *tôrah*) for humankind, but a radically new integration of those laws into the essential being of the human, what he calls "a new covenant" (Jeremiah 31:31–34). Ezekiel has a vivid metaphor for a generation acquainted (as is ours) with heart transplant surgery: "I will remove from your body the heart of stone and give you a heart of flesh" (Ezekiel 36:26b). As many people living today owe their new lease on life to the medical pioneering of doctors like Christiaan Barnard, so too Ezekiel in his day delivered the Divine Surgeon's assurance that they too could enjoy the new life of communion with God and compassion to their neighbors.

As much as a contemporary generation would like to have access to a more nonchalant *vade mecum* in dealing with human defects, the Christian message is no less emphatic today than in Ezekiel's or Paul's time in insisting that repentance and a completely new life orientation can be the only authentic response in a situation where government and commerce are being degraded by corruption and greed, nations are set against nations by aggression and distrust, and personal lives are afflicted by lack of integrity and generosity, and, moreover, where the prevailing economic and political answers being produced by parties clamoring for control of governments throughout the world are pathetically incapable of arresting serious spirals of decline.

Unfortunately, humans are endlessly resourceful in evading responsibility and downplaying the seriousness of the human condition. While maintaining a lifestyle predicated on the assumption of entitlement to vastly more of the earth's resources than the average fellow human, we are in denial about how this is connected to the degradation of our (God's!) natural environment. To maintain a geopolitical and economic situation beneficial to our self-interests, we initiate military interventions that are hard to justify by anyone upholding the value of life of a family in Baghdad or Gaza as equal to our own. Poverty weighs like a leaden yoke on an increasing percentage of the world's population while we perfect our myopia to the degree of not feeling the pain of an undernourished child in Madras or Mogadishu. Economists are able to defend a certain level of unemployment as essential for the economy with an economic statistic drained of any human dimension. Substandard wages, anemic national health insurance policy, and hazardous working conditions are defended as an inevitable consequence of global competition, in regard to which we are to be so pleased with abundant and low-cost merchandise that the consequences in human misery of laissez-faire capitalism are overlooked. The agricultural industry is revolutionized by huge agribusinesses enjoying government subsidies, while increasing numbers of family farmers are driven to despair and even suicide out of the shame accompanying loss of ancestral land. On all levels of society and the economy, political leaders and academic theorists look to solutions predicated on economic theories and implemented by advanced technology. As important as is such input in a complex world, essential elements in any lasting improvement are sacrificed if the world is not acknowledged as a divine gift and if human dignity is not vouched safe by recognition of the divine image in every human being.

It would be naive to deny that Christians must be full participants in every human agency charged with applying the finest intellectual and material resources available to improve the quality of life of humans throughout the world. But our most unique contribution is lost if we do not look more deeply to see the world as Christ saw it. We have to see our role in addressing political and economic problems as distinct from one viewing them strictly through the lens of social or political or natural science. Our particular contribution to the public good is preserved only if we point out that human problems such as hunger and poverty are more than economic problems, for they manifest dislocations at the heart of the human family, which is to say that on the most basic level they are spiritual problems. Neglect of the poor becomes more than a campaign issue; it is unmasked as an affront to the One who died for the hungry and neglected of society. Only when apathy toward the millions in the world who are starving and wasting away from disease is recognized as the product of the heart's hardening is there hope that a transformation will occur that is capable of radically changing both personal lifestyles and national priorities.

The repeated failures of "solutions" based solely on economic theory and new approaches to production and distribution point to the inadequacy of strictly human approaches. Not merely new initiatives, but a re-envisioning of the human condition is mandated, one arising from a view of all persons as God's children belonging to one interdependent family. Only when change begins with conversion of the heart will abstract construals of human problems yield to the palpably human understanding in which the rape victim of Darfur is a sister, the amputee in Baghdad an uncle, the beggar in a Manila street and the prisoner in Guantanamo Bay a member of the family circle. It is time for Christians to awaken to the significance of adding to economic and technological theory the understanding of humans not simply in terms of producer and consumer, but as children of one God and members of a global family bearing responsibility for each other and for their natural environment. Poverty, hunger, disease, and war are not simply earthly problems from which Christians pray to be spared. They are signs of a broken covenant, a fracturing of the very universe that God has created, and the ruinous effects are ones in which we are implicated. We must learn to stand in solidarity with the victims of a degraded environment and with those impoverished by the greed of wealthy nations and multinational corporations if we are to participate in the hope that transcends and is capable of vanquishing futility.

In repentance acknowledging our own contribution to the brokenness of creation and in solidarity taking our position with rather than above the victims of oppression and abuse, we embody the first part of the biblical dialectical understanding of the human condition, captured by Paul in the phrase "given up to futility." Without taking this step into the radical realism of the Bible, we cannot enter into the hope beyond futility without compromising the Gospel via escapism, triumphalism, absolutism, or other forms of whittling God down to human size. Chastened by full acknowledgement of the futility of a self-contained human existence and turning to God in faith, however, the pilgrim of faith dares to enter into the hope of a creation, while fallen, yet yearning for restoration to wholeness, a hope that is not passive but which draws us as participating agents in the very lives we live in our concrete vocations.

A final obstacle, however, hovers over the path of that pilgrim. It comes in the form of an intellectual challenge and takes aim precisely at the hope that sustains the Christian: "For all of your claiming to be a realist, your living 'in hope' of the final healing of creation reveals your true colors as a dreaming Utopian." Christians are not able to refute this claim on the terms set by the interlocutor, for Christian discourse is not predicated on "scientific" analysis but on truthful testimony. Therefore, we point to the One in whose foot steps we walk, One who did not deny the crushing impact of evil upon human frailty, but in a moment of anguish gave expression to his sense of abandonment, "My God, my God, why have you forsaken me" (Matthew 27:46 // Mark 15:34). It is noteworthy that at the point of death, Jesus addressed God not with the more personal epithets of Abba or Lord, but as God, that is to say, the Holy One, the Almighty, the Creator of Heaven and Earth, the one to whom he had single-heartedly devoted his every effort and to whom he now surrendered his life under the harshest imaginable circumstances. In response to the cultured despiser of Christianity, therefore, we offer not "proofs" but testimony, for we encounter in Jesus not a "dreaming Utopian," but a faithful servant devoted to the ones he came to serve right up to his last gasping breath.

We take a shortcut to the ultimate hope of biblical faith for the human condition if we do not accept Christ's anguished cry of doubt and despair as the inseparable companion of hope, or to use a familiar biblical metaphor, as the birth pangs of a new creation. From our perspective, the problems of the world are overwhelmingly disproportionate to our human resources. That is why the hope to which we are directed in faith is neither dreaming utopianism nor overconfidence in human capabilities. It is hope that participates fully in the dialectical view of the human condition we have found in the Bible. In the words of the Apostle Paul: "Now hope that is seen is not hope. For who hopes for what is seen? But if we hope for what we do not see, we wait for it with patience" (Romans 8:24–25).

In the vividness of the Gospel narrative, we discover the nature of the hope that moves steadfastly toward what is yet unseen without falling into the nefariousness of Utopia. The key to this balance between realism and hope is solidarity with the neglected— yes, the wretched of the earth, the starving, the imprisoned, the friendless—a solidarity predicated not on sentiment but on kinship. And for Christians, that solidarity comes though identification with Jesus Christ Savior. Granted, modern examples of Christian solidarity with the poor and forgotten are few. But we are not left without guidance, for we cannot avoid the picture of Mother Teresa embracing the untouchables of Calcutta, nor can we deny that the unbroken sisterhood reaching from Jesus to Teresa continues in AIDS clinics throughout the world and in prison ministries and in homeless shelters. With these examples vividly in mind, we must answer the question facing every Christian in today's world: "Will we preserve in our personal lives and communities the testimony of such examples of the way of the servant Christ, or will we allow our vision to be distracted by the secular world's denial of Christ's abiding presence and its reduction of realism to the existential emptiness described over a century ago by Stephen Crane:

> A man said to the universe,
> "Sir, I exist!"
> "However," replied the universe,
> "The fact has not created in me
> A sense of obligation."[11]

For the Christian, the manifestations of the brokenness of humanity are as many and as real as for anyone else. The difference lies alone in the Good News that is the heart of the Gospel, that in the life of Christ and in the dwelling of Christ's Spirit within and among us, we can experience in our daily lives the unfolding of the promise that God is at work healing the world as we participate in that healing in touching with God's love our families, our extended family in the church, and most especially the ones closest to the heart of Christ, "the least of these, my sisters and brothers."

The healing and renewal of life extended to the world by God in Jesus Christ Savior is often described in the Bible as a "new covenant." The reality of that covenant in the midst of our troubled world becomes palpable to us as we extend our hands to receive Christ's gifts in the Eucharist and hear the marvelous words, "this is the new covenant in my blood . . ." The Apostle Paul describes the new covenant in 2 Corinthians 5 in terms of new creation born of reconciliation, humans re-connecting with each other because they have been re-connected to their God through Christ: "So if anyone is in Christ, there is a new creation: everything old has passed away; see, everything has become new. All this is from God, who reconciled us to himself through Christ, and has given us the ministry of reconciliation; that is, in Christ God was reconciling the world to himself, not counting their trespasses against them, and entrusting the message of reconciliation to us. So we are ambassadors for Christ, since God is making His appeal through us; we entreat you on behalf of Christ, be reconciled to God" (2 Corinthians 5:17–20).

11. Crane, "Poem 21," in *War is Kind and Other Lines.*

In this passage, the Apostle Paul has heightened the dialectic at the center of the biblical view of reality to its limit. The old to which he refers is the inscrutable perversity of the human heart that was described by Jeremiah and Paul himself. But here, he announces that the old "has passed away, see everything has become new." That is the Good News of the Gospel. That is the proclamation of God's audacity resulting not from some economic tinkering and social engineering so that life will be a little better for a few more people; no, it results from a new reality that replaces the old. The radical break here is nothing less than the passing of one era and the beginning of a new one. The temptation facing those called to be ambassadors of this hope is to be engulfed by the drab cynicism of the world, "Christian hope is merely wishful thinking," or in Karl Marx's metaphor, an "opium" to keep the suffering masses in a submissive stupor. Unfortunately, Marx had seen clearly that powerful capitalists in his time were eager to use religion to pacify the workers they exploited, and he extrapolated from that his universal explanation of religion.

But Paul was speaking not of an opiate, but of a profound truth that opens the eyes of human beings toward each other and empowers them to become agents of the new era, in which all that oppresses and demeans life will be replaced by the reign of God's righteousness. The event that inaugurates that new era is not a mystical technique, it is not a new therapeutic method, it is not even a seven-point economic program. It is, rather, God's triumph over life's enemies accomplished in the life, death and resurrection of our Lord. What is its scope? It is the entire universe. Where does it begin? In the conversion and the commissioning of the individual believer. This starting point in the life of the individual is an aspect of the Gospel with which many modern, and especially liberal Christians feel uncomfortable. Paul does not pander to modern squeamishness over the radical language of conversion. In Galatians 2:19–20, he gives his personal testimony: "I have been crucified with Christ. It is no longer I who live but it is Christ who lives in me." This is the same Paul who, in Romans, gives expression to his despair over his human potential for good: "For I know that nothing good dwells within me, that is, in my flesh. I can will what is right, but I cannot do it" (Romans 7:18). The dialectic lying at the heart of the biblical understanding of the human condition could not be drawn more clearly. Powerless by himself, Paul relies entirely on God's power coming through his identification with Christ in his death and resurrection.

Beginning with his rebirth in Christ, conversion for Paul breaks the bounds of a private transaction. What takes root in the heart goes public as part of an event encompassing the human family, for "God who reconciled us to himself through Christ . . . has given us the ministry of reconciliation" (2 Corinthians 5:18). Reconciliation, as the process of healing all that is broken in the world, cannot be separated from the proclamation of what God has done in Christ to reconcile each of us to God, nor can it be separated from what God continues to do though our "ministry of reconciliation" in relation to hunger, poverty, corruption, and failed government policies. And the ministry to which we belong must not be confused with replacing one failed self-help program with another, nor with human efforts to establish prosperity through economic engineering, nor with geo-political strategies for peace through the unilateral imposition of democracy on intractable nations. It is not promulgating a purported universal philosophy of justice and liberty, as impressive as such intellectual exercises are in the hands of a Kant or Rawls. It begins not with such human programs, but with God's act, already accomplished in Christ, of reconciling humans to one another as the starting point for a healing process into which we are drawn. As humans, we have a vast array of different vocations, but in Christ, we are called to devote our vocations to the higher calling of being agents of God's reconciling the world to himself. By accepting God's initiating act on our behalf as the starting point of anything we wish to accomplish in the world, we accept God's plan for reality as the basis for utilizing the best that modern science and technology can provide for addressing epidemic diseases, hunger, and international conflict, and for cooperating with all who are devoted to justice and peace, whatever their own philosophical or religious starting points may be.

Collectively, Paul calls Christ's ambassadors of reconciliation the "Body of Christ," a very concrete way of stating that the church is in the world to continue the work that Jesus Christ began. As the church was born through God's gracious gift in Christ, so too it is sustained by the extension of that gift in time through the sacraments. In baptism, the believer is drawn into unity with Christ, and thereby rescued from death and made a part of the new creation. And in the Eucharist, we celebrate proleptically God's universal reign of compassionate justice and peace. To be sure, our gathering falls far short of the entirety of restored creation, but in the way we treat one another with forgiveness and tender care, we are part of a drama that will not end until all of God's children, rich, poor, powerful and weak are united as one loving family. And the reach of that redemptive drama even goes further . . .

In Romans 8:18–39, the Apostle Paul strains the capacity of human language to express the breadth and depth of the Christian hope for reconciliation. Nothing could state more clearly that his God was not one whittled down to a size fitting the needs of introspective individuals fretting over their personal salvation, but a God whose care embraced the entire creation. He witnesses the "eager longing" for freedom from bondage and redemption shared by the children of God in the company of all creation. The image is one that stretches the imagination of faith until all gods fashioned after a human likeness are demolished and the mind is reopened to the true God whose stature over-arches even as it nurtures and sustains an expanding universe so stupendous that it can be fathomed only in the language of praise. It also secures, as the context of Christian participation in God's redemptive drama, solidarity with all God's children, with the entire human race, and finally, with the entire universe.

Having allowed the razor of Scripture to cut out of our consciousness the puny gods of our own making, we find that same Scripture inscribing on our hearts a fervent love for a God so vast as to embrace the cosmos in one redemptive purpose, and yet so close as to invite us to continue the healing work of Jesus Christ Savior in the power of his Spirit. One aspect of the freedom found in that service is freedom from the pathetic image of a god equivalent to a genie in a bottle carried around by its owner and ready on command to provide an escape from harm. How interesting it is that the Apostle Paul found *personal* assurance precisely within the context of the drama of *cosmic* redemption, where hopelessness over the human condition and anxiety over personal salvation where both overwhelmed by the immeasurable love of God witnessed in the life of Jesus Christ: "For I am convinced that neither death, nor life, nor angels, nor rulers, nor things present, nor things to come, nor powers, nor height, nor depth, nor anything else in all creation, will be able to separate us from the love of God in Christ Jesus our Lord" (Romans 8:38–39).

5 Old Problems, New Opportunities

"The imperative of the moment is to change fundamentally our approach to the world."[1] This is the conclusion Boston University professor Andrew Bacevich draws after subjecting the policies of George W. Bush's administration to a scathing critique based on the writings of Reinhold Niebuhr. Niebuhr had warned that four fatal flaws in self-perception tracing back to the ideological foundations of the nation persistently shape the United States into a menace on the world scene even as it perceives itself as God's appointed special agent for world order: "American Exceptionalism, the indecipherability of history, the false allure of simple solutions, and . . . the imperative of appreciating the limits of power."[2] In a tragic paralleling of the policy adopted by Lyndon Johnson in dealing with the purported threat of Communism's Southeast Asian beachhead towards world domination, the Bush Doctrine portrayed the war in Iraq as the necessary measure to stop the worldwide threat of terrorism, the consequences of which were previewed on September 11, 2001. And even as the war against godless Communism was a spiritual crusade, so too the war on terrorism, while responding to national security and economic interests, is a part of a larger historical pattern "set by liberty and the Author of liberty."[3]

The identification of U.S. international policy with divine purpose is lodged at the heart of the American epic. At times when that policy is flourishing, such as the culminating months of World War II or during the final stages of the collapse of the Soviet Union, criticism of "manifest destiny" is denounced as not only unpatriotic but sacrilegious. In darker days of U.S. foreign involvement, how-

1. Bacevich, "Prophets and Poseurs," 36.
2. Ibid, 27.
3. George W. Bush, Second Inaugural Address, January 20, 2005.

ever, sinister icons such as the helicopter evacuation of Ambassador Graham Martin from the American embassy in Saigon in 1975 or the publication in 2004 of portraits of torture victims in the Abu Ghraib prison create a climate more open to introspection and self-criticism. Words such as the following, also from George W. Bush's Second Inaugural, are scrutinized anew: "America's vital interests and our deepest beliefs are now one ... We go forward with complete confidence in the eventual triumph of freedom." Granting that the conduct of the Iraq war is reflective of the "deepest beliefs" of some citizens (including the former President), what is to be concluded regarding the nature of those beliefs? Reinhold Niebuhr would name such faith *nationalistic idolatry.* Andrew Bacevich agrees. So do I.

A serious response is owed to those who regard such a critical assessment to be unfair, unpatriotic, or even un-Christian, for the temptation to invoke divine authority in defense of partisan political views threatens to ensnare liberals and conservatives alike. Moreover, the best safeguard against self-deception and false certainty is open debate between opposing viewpoints within all segments of a society. Rather than hurling one set of absolute assertions to refute another set, the person or community of faith seeking to warn against the exploitation of religion for propagandistic purposes must provide a careful exposition of Jewish and Christian Scripture and tradition to demonstrate the relevance for national policy of the central biblical confession that there exists only one absolute Authority in the universe, and that the legitimacy of any government derives solely from the degree to which the laws and policies of that government conform to the moral principles that can be inferred from God's nature and God's rule over creation. Many thoughtful people, including people of faith, in considering the daunting nature of that challenge, choose the cautious path of defining religion as a personal matter and limiting the realm of government to procedures shaped by secular arguments and objectives. That alternative may be capable of preserving order in normal times and among communities of fair-minded citizens, but sole reliance on the secular premises of a political regime becomes dangerous in proportion to that regime's ability to consolidate power and to monopolize public discourse. This is not to deny the dangers inherent in opening public debate to religious themes, for the debilitating effects of arguments claiming a divine authority that trumps all other arguments are well known in our society. But the misuse of religious argument is not effectively addressed by banning religion from the public forum, for such a move simply privileges one perspective over the other, that is, the secular over the religious. Rather, what is required of all participants constituting a diverse society is respect for basic rules of civility, including openness to differing viewpoints and dedication to reasonable discussion leading to definition of common goals and the strategies capable of reaching them. Beyond this those who choose to take an active part in political process must trust that their society is sufficiently endowed with the wisdom and historical consciousness capable of distinguishing reasonable argument from irrational fanaticism and sheer delusion.

The position of Reinhold Niebuhr, tested in the crucible of international crisis and weathering the test of time, is one that must be taken seriously in any contemporary discussion regarding governmental authority and the framework within which nations deal with international conflict. One particularly poignant principle developed in Niebuhr's political thought that is firmly rooted in Jewish and Christian Scripture applies to human institutions: the confession that there is only one Sovereign of the universe to whom humans owe unqualified allegiance and obedience. It denounces the claim of any nation to possess the unilateral right and authority to determine the destinies of other nations or to take exception to the limits imposed by the world community on the exercise of power by any one state.[4] Given the complexity of most political problems, the

---

4. The centrality of the confession of God's sole sovereignty and the political inference arising from this confession, namely, the relativization of all earthly authorities, comes to clarity through careful, thorough biblical study. The implications of the first commandment for the construction of political institutions emerged within the faith of ancient Israel amidst bitter struggle, especially between kings and prophets. There is no denying that in certain passages of the Bible robust claims are made on behalf of the rights and privileges of kings that in the history of the West have been used as warrants to justify the concept of the divine right of kings. Verses 1–37 of Psalm 89 present an especially high notion of the special status the Davidic king enjoys

elusiveness of effective strategies and policies, and the infinite categorical distinction between the mind of God and the knowledge of humans, a further inference follows, namely that international crises must be approached by world leaders in a spirit of cooperation and sensitivity to differing perspectives and interests. Furthermore, patience in debate must stand firm against the temptation of those with the greatest power to impose solutions.

Sadly, the approach taken by the U.S. administration in the early years of the new millennium to the complicated issues being debated within the United Nations contradicted the teachings outlined by Niebuhr, teachings solidly based on Niebuhr's profound understanding of the central tenets of Scripture. The choice to withdraw from open, international dialogue and embark unilaterally on a military initiative was articulated in September 2001 by President Bush, "Every nation, in every region, now has a decision to make. Either you are with us, or you are with the terrorists."[5] And given the President's religious conviction that he was following divine direction in his conduct of foreign policy, the implication is clear: "In deciding whether or not to join our coalition, you are choosing either to be on God's side, or Satan's." In this theo-political pattern of thought, the younger Bush was following the example of his father

---

in his covenantal relationship with God. The last fifteen verses of that same Psalm, however, indicate how the travails of history shook the confidence of those adhering to this notion of royal authority. One of the primary themes within the history of biblical prophecy is the repudiation of the tendency of kingship to claim for itself a status and authority that the prophets professed belonged to God alone. The limited, penultimate nature of royal authority and the obligation to be faithful to the Torah that the king shares with his subjects was codified into law in Deuteronomy 17:14–20. The abiding relevance of that law becomes evident in the terms used by scholars to describe its underlying political principle, terms such as "limited" or "constitutional" monarchy.

5. Quoted from George W. Bush's address to a joint session of Congress on September 20, 2001. That the basic topos "if not for... against" traces back to words of Jesus in Matthew 12:30 does not justify its blithe political application, but rather underscores the reckless arrogance underlying such a blustering throwing down of the gauntlet. It is sobering to note that at the height of their power, Lenin and Mussolini presented to the nations of the world the same choice, a fact not forgotten by the European leaders of the post-Cold War period and one that should be deeply troubling to Americans.

(though it should be noted that the elder Bush adopted a surprisingly critical position vis-à-vis his son's Iraq policy). In reference to the encouragement he had gotten from Billy Graham and other Evangelical leaders to launch operation Desert Storm in 1991, George H. W. Bush later expressed his gratitude: "I want to thank you for helping America, as Christ ordained, to be a light unto the world."[6] I believe that is accurate to conclude that with a statement of certainty like that, the President crossed a line that Reinhold Niebuhr would have attacked as politically hazardous. And theologically, it adheres to the type of nationalistic hubris that the Hebrew prophets denounced as idolatrous.

Our interlocutor, the defender of the notion that the United States has a divine calling to spread freedom and democracy to all the nations of the world, may retort, "On what basis do you question the special sacred trust conferred by God upon our nation? Do you not contradict your own premise that all human understanding is fallible when you claim the support of the biblical prophets for your political views?" These questions are legitimate, and if offered sincerely can open up constructive dialogue, the kind that can safeguard all participants from irrational absolutism. An honest response to those believing that they were being true both to country and faith in embracing the notion of divine calling conveyed by epithets like "the new Israel," "God's agent in spreading democracy and restoring world order," and "Christ's light to the world" could take the form of a question: Does that notion stand in tension with the First Commandment and the biblical picture of God's evenhanded concern for all nations?[7] The biblical discussion could then be supplemented with examples of courageous religious leaders like Dietrich Bonhoeffer, Martin Luther King Jr., and Oscar Romero who dared to oppose nationalistic idolatry and sealed their witness with martyrs' blood. At the same time, it would be important to point out that these modern saints took their stands with fear and trembling, ever aware that moral certainty is beyond the reach of humans, ever seeking to test their political strategies within the con-

6. Quoted in Andrew Rosenthal, "In a Speech, President Returns to Religious Themes."

7. Cf. Amos 9:7–8.

text of communal worship, prayer, and study, and never expecting ultimate triumph in this world's imperfect order. Above all, though, the point would be made that in daring to criticize their nation's leaders, Bonhoeffer, King, and Romero were not being unpatriotic, but rather were expressing their profound love of homeland by remaining loyal, first and foremost, to their God.

While seeking to avoid a liberal version of absolutism and arrogance, I have, in the chapters of this book, sought to identify biblical themes that constitute a reliable foundation for a critique of nationalistic idolatry and that form a sound basis for a morally responsible national self-understanding. I have sought to show how people of faith can engage in political discourse without violating the rights of fellow citizens and can contribute to international debates in a manner open to and respectful of other faiths, political philosophies and national interests. I have described how believers can clarify their starting point through faithfulness in worship, how they can gain insight into the intractable problems facing every generation through open discussion, first in the language of their particular tradition within congregational forums, and then in public discussion enabled by careful cultivation of an appropriate theo-political hermeneutic. I have drawn on H. Richard Niebuhr to call attention to the importance of the biblical concept of covenant in reestablishing public trust, unity, and honesty. And I have sought to expose the self-indulgent and self-serving contemporary image of Jesus Christ as personal patron of privileged individuals and their chosen homeland to the Jesus Christ of the Bible whose concern over the human condition reaches out to every clan and nation.

But how do such theological exercises address the critical domestic and international issues that threaten to destroy civilization and the human values we associate with decent societies? Emphatically, they do not supply apodictic answers that can be fetched from Scripture or a particular denomination's teachings and imposed on a nation or world. Rather, they are to be viewed as tutorials in cultivating a civic consciousness capable of political engagement that is at once faithful to one's spiritual legacy, self-critical and open to other points of view, and dedicated to the equality and well-being of all humans within their particular communities and nations. Or to state the matter even more audaciously in the words of Andrew Bacevich, they can contribute to "the imperative of the moment," "to change fundamentally our approach to the world."[8]

Bacevich's article was written before the inauguration of Barack Obama as the 44th President of the United States of America. Obama's campaign accentuated precisely the theme of *change*. In the wake of the November 4, 2008, election, many supporters of the new administration declared that a new era had arrived, and they began predicting sweeping changes in health insurance, foreign policy, and human rights. Has the call for fundamental change been answered?

Though heartened by the policies of the new president and encouraged both by the new composition of the chambers of Congress and by well-vetted, credible cabinet and judicial appointments, I remain sanguine about the prospects for comprehensive change in key policies. The struggle for a humane society will continue. The need for watchfulness on the part of religious communities and people of faith remains as urgent as ever. This cautiously hopeful position stems from the Niebuhrian realism that I share with scholars like Bacevich, according to which it is a categorical error to confuse any human regime with Utopia or the Messianic kingdom.

While many people of faith, including myself, believe that the moral credibility of the United States in the eyes of the world has improved since the 2008 election and see signs that areas such as health care and the economy are beginning to receive the attention they deserve, the prophetic voices must be heeded that warn that the fundamental challenge facing those who acknowledge only one ultimate Authority in the universe and subject all leaders and governments and their policies to the moral principles inferred from that Authority's rule remains unchanged. That challenge revolves around cultivating a basis upon which to detect and oppose all forms of nationalistic hubris and idolatry and bringing to clarity an understanding of the proper role of a powerful, wealthy nation in opposing inequality and injustice, contributing to the health and prosperity of all its citizens, being an instrument of peace among

8. Bacevich, "Prophets and Poseurs."

all nations, and being more eager to rectify wrongs at home than to impose its cultural values and political policies abroad.

Now as ever, people and communities of faith must steadfastly attend to the cultivation of the qualities of character that enable them to contribute to the vitality and humaneness of their nation. Now as ever, faithfulness in worship and participation in critical reflection and compassionate action are essential parts of congregational life. Political involvement will not lead to parceling out expert advice in all areas of life. With humility and a sense of the scientific, political, and economic complexity of the crises that face our generation, believers will be clear as to their limited role in the myriad issues facing modern societies. But humility does not imply withdrawal from the fray, for the ultimate authority of God, precisely in its repudiation of the claim of any nation to special privilege, is the source of the mandate incumbent upon religious communities to witness non-triumphantly, but steadfastly and with courage, to justice and compassion in a world torn by hunger, disease, and conflict.

The nature of the challenge facing faith communities can be illustrated with reference to two contemporary problems, one international and the other domestic.

In the area of international relations, commentators have noted that Afghanistan has the potential to emerge as President Obama's Iraq. In the face of the recurrence of the issues of safe havens for terrorist groups and the potential of regional tensions to flare up into nuclear-fed international conflict, we are hearing the call by military leaders for a substantial increase in ground forces in that beleaguered region of the world. To issue a categorical repudiation of Pentagon deployment strategies would be a blatant example of religious communities claiming expertise in areas where they lack requisite credentials. But this is not to obscure the legitimacy of another type of dialogical engagement, one emerging directly from the perspective of those obedient to the God whose love extends equally to all humans and nations, an engagement that raises the critical question of the limits of military power and warns against the temptation to exercise dominion over other peoples by unilaterally imposing solutions. To think that the seduction of superior power has lost its appeal as the result of one election is to abandon the prophetic attentiveness incumbent upon every community dedicated to universal justice, peace and prosperity. At the same time, the critique of policies based primarily on military might must only be preparatory to emphasizing more humane and effective strategies, strategies predicated on the belief that for change to be lasting it must place emphasis on health care, nutrition, education and economic development, even as it pays respectful attention to the perceived priorities and needs of indigenous leaders and populations.

In the area of domestic issues, the United States has entered its most promising opportunity to improve the quality of health care for all of its citizens since the first years of the Clinton presidency. In 1993 the newly elected President, with the active participation of his wife, advanced a plan intended to secure universal health insurance. The plan failed to gain traction, in no small part due to the lobbying efforts of pharmaceutical firms and medical associations smarting from a sense of being excluded from the process and determined to safeguard their self-interests. During the new round of debates on health care, for faith communities to be seduced by claims that in the new era of change corporate greed and professional self-interest have yielded to good will and beneficent attentiveness to the poor and underserved would be to abandon their moral responsibility to advocate for those who have neither sufficient means nor clout to defend their rights to affordable health care and occupational opportunity.

Chastened by the lessons of history, President Obama has sought to be bipartisan and inclusive of all interested sectors in his approach to healthcare reform, but the path to success remains riddled with obstacles. In this domestic area as in international relations, faith as such does not produce solutions to the highly complex scientific, economic, and social dimensions implicated in the delivery of effective health services to all citizens. But the perspective of faith does contribute to an important dimension in the debate, the moral dimension, and this, once again, in both a critical and a positive sense. Prophetic critique is called for in response to a human trait that once again raises its ugly head, greed, both in individual and in corporate form. Faith communities must remind the their fellow citizens that "to the least of these . . ." is not a matter of religious conscience alone, but points to the political mandate ensconced in the founding documents of our nation and incumbent upon every legitimate government to uphold its obligation to foster and preserve the health and well-being of *all* of its citizens, whether they be rich or poor, represented or underrepresented, majority or minority, male or female, young or old, firm or infirm.

On the positive side of the health care debate, communities of faith will attest to the long-range benefits to the nation as a whole that derive from the cultivation of *shalom*, for from the care and healing of all its citizens arise a social soundness that becomes the basis not only for improved national health, but for social accord and political vitality that enable a people to move beyond self-interest by contributing robustly to other members of the family of nations in their struggles with the debilitating effects of HIV/AIDs, hunger, regional conflict, abuse of women, and the threat of terrorism. While remaining realistic about the limited potential of governments and other human institutions, decent people of all faiths and persuasions share in the joy of even partial glimpses of the day when

> Steadfast love and faithfulness will meet;
>> righteousness and peace will kiss each other. (Psalm 85:10)

Bibliography

Bacevich, Andrew J. "Prophets and Poseurs: Niebuhr and Our Times." *World Affairs* (Winter 2008) 27–36. Online: http://www.worldaffairsjournal.org/2008%20-%20Winter/full-prophets.html.

Baltzer, Klaus. *The Covenant Formulary in Old Testament, Jewish and Early Christian Writings.* Translated by David E. Green. Philadelphia: Fortress, 1971.

Barr, James. "Abba Isn't Daddy." *Journal of Theological Studies* 39 (1988) 28–47.

Bellah, Robert N. *The Broken Covenant: American Civil Religion in Time of Trial.* New York: Seabury, 1975.

Bellah, Robert N. et al. *The Good Society.* New York: Knopf, 1991.

———. *Habits of the Heart: Individualism and Commitment in American Life.* New York: Harper & Row, 1985.

Bethge, Eberhard. *Dietrich Bonhoeffer: Eine Biographie.* Munich: Kaiser 1967.

———. *Dietrich Bonhoeffer: A Biography.* Translated by Eric Mosbacher et al. Revised and edited by Victoria J. Barnett. Minneapolis: Fortress, 2000.

Beveridge, Albert. Speech delivered on January 9, 1900. Online: encarta.msn.com/sidebar_761594590/Senator_Beveridge_on_Imperialism.html

Bloom, Allan David. *The Closing of the American Mind.* New York: Simon & Schuster, 1987.

Bonhoeffer, Dietrich. *The Cost of Discipleship.* Translated by Reginald H. Fuller. New York: Macmillan, 1949.

Bush, George H. W. Remarks at the Annual Convention of National Religious Broadcasters, January 27, 1992. Online: http://bushlibrary.tamu.edu/research/public_papers.php?id=3882&year=1992&month=0.

Bush, George H. W., and Brent Scowcroft. *A World Transformed.* New York: Knopf, 1998.

Cassidy, Richard J. *Paul in Chains: Roman Imprisonment and the Letters of St. Paul.* New York: Crossroad, 2001.

Crane, Stephen. *War Is Kind and Other Lines.* New York: Stokes, 1899.

Eichrodt, Walther. "Prophet and Covenant: Observations on the Exegesis of Isaiah." In *Proclamation and Presence: Old Testament Essays in Honor of Gwynne Henton Davies,* ed. John I. Durham and J. R. Porter, 167–88. Richmond: John Knox, 1970.

Bibliography

Frankfort, Henri. *Kingship and the Gods: A Study of Ancient Near Eastern Religion as the Integration of Society and Nature*. Chicago: University of Chicago Press, 1948.

Hanson, Paul D. *Old Testament Apocalyptic*. Nashville: Abingdon, 1987.

———. *The People Called: The Growth of Community in the Bible*. 2nd ed. Louisville: Westminster John Knox, 2001.

———. "Worship: Touchstone of Christian Political Action." In *Religion and Politics: (Mis)Interpreting the Bible*, 31–55. Manila: CBAP, 2006.

Hauerwas, Stanley. *Performing the Faith*. Grand Rapids: Brasos, 2004.

Hillers, Delbert R. *Covenant: The History of a Biblical Idea*. Baltimore: Johns Hopkins University Press, 1969.

Hunter, James Davison. *Culture Wars: The Struggle to Define America*. New York: Basic Books, 1991.

Huntingdon, Samuel. *The Clash of Civilizations and the Remaking of World Order*. New York: Simon & Schuster, 1996.

Kant, Immanuel. *Critique of Pure Reason*. Translated by Norman Kemp Smith. New York: St. Martin's, 1965.

Kierkegaard, Søren. *Either/Or*. 2 vols. Translated by Walter Lowrie. Garden City, NY: Doubleday, 1959.

———. *Fear and Trembling and The Book on Adler*. Translated by Walter Lowrie. New York: Knopf, 1994.

———. *Training in Christianity*. Translated by Walter Lowrie. Princeton: Princeton University Press, 1944.

LaHaye, Tim. *Mind Siege: The Battle for Truth in the New Millennium*. Nashville: Word, 2000.

Leclerc, Thomas L. *Yahweh Is Exalted in Justice: Solidarity and Conflict in Isaiah*. Minneapolis: Fortress, 2001.

Lehman, Paul. *Ethics in a Christian Context*. New York: Harper & Row, 1963.

Levine, Amy-Jill. "Jesus and Judaism: Why the Connection Still Matters." In *Ethical Dimensions in the Teaching of Jesus and Paul*, 64–66. Manila: CBAP, 2005.

Lindsell, Harold. *The Battle for the Bible*. Grand Rapids: Zondervan, 1976.

Lindsey, Hal, with C. C. Carlson. *The Late Great Planet Earth*. Grand Rapids: Zondervan, 1970.

Locke, John. *Two Treatises of Government*. 1690.

Luo, Michael. "Preaching a Gospel of Wealth in a Glittery Market, New York." *New York Times* (15 January 2006).

MacIntyre, Alasdair. *After Virtue: A Study in Moral Theory*. Notre Dame, IN: University of Notre Dame Press, 1981.

McBride, S. Dean. "Polity of the Covenant People: The Book of Deuteronomy." *Interpretation* 41 (1987) 229–44.

McCarthy, Dennis J., SJ. *Treaty and Covenant: A Study in Form in the Ancient Oriental Documents and in the Old Testament.* 2nd ed. AnBib 21; Rome: Pontifical Biblical Institute Press, 1978.

Mendenhall, George E. *Law and Covenant in Israel and the Ancient Near East.* Pittsburgh: Biblical Colloquium, 1955.

National Conference of Catholic Bishops. *Economic Justice for All: Pastoral Letter on Catholic Social Teaching and the U.S. Economy.* 10th anniversary ed. Washington, DC: United States Catholic Conference, 1997.

Nicholson, Ernest W. *God and His People: Covenant and Theology in the Old Testament.* Oxford: Clarendon, 1986.

Niebuhr, H. Richard. "The Idea of Covenant and American Democracy." *Church History* 23 (1954) 126–35.

Nietzsche, Friedrich. "The Genealogy of Morals." In *The Philosophy of Nietzsche,* 617–807. Translated by Horace B. Samuel. New York: Modern Library, 1954.

O'Sullivan, John L. "The Great Nation of Futurity." *The United States Democratic Review* 6/23 (1839) 426–30. Online: http://www.mtholyoke.edu/acad/intrel/osulliva.htm.

Otto, Rudolf. *The Idea of the Holy: An Inquiry into the Non-rational Factor in the Idea of the Divine and Its Relation to the Rational.* 2nd ed. Translated by John W. Harvey. New York: Oxford University Press, 1958.

Perlitt, Lothar. *Bundestheologie im Alten Testament.* Wissenschaftliche Monographien zum Alten und Neuen Testament 36. Neukirchen-Vluyn: Neukirchener, 1969.

Putnam, Robert D. *Bowling Alone: The Collapse and Revival of American Community.* New York: Simon & Schuster 2000.

Rawls, John. *Political Liberalism.* New York: Columbia University Press, 1993.

———. *A Theory of Justice.* Cambridge: Harvard University Press, 1971.

Richley, A. James. *Religion in American Public Life.* Washington, DC: Brookings Institute Press, 1985.

Roberts, J. J. M. "Isaiah in Old Testament Theology." In *Interpreting the Prophets,* edited by James L. Mays and Paul Achtemeier, 62–74. Philadelphia: Fortress, 1987.

Rorty, Richard. "Religion as Conversation-stopper." In *Philosophy and Social Hope,* 168–74. New York: Penguin, 1999.

Rosenthal, Andrew. "In a Speech, President Returns to Religious Themes." *New York Times,* January 28, 1992, A17.

Sandel, Michael J. *Democracy's Discontent: America in Search of a Public Philosophy.* Cambridge: Harvard University Press, 1996.

Bibliography

————. "The Procedural Republic and the Unencumbered Self." In *Contemporary Political Philosophy: An Anthology*, edited by Robert E. Goodin and Philip Pettit, 247–55. Oxford: Blackwell, 1997.

Seitz, Christopher R., editor. *Reading and Preaching the Book of Isaiah*. Philadelphia: Fortress, 1988.

Smart, James D. *The Strange Silence of the Bible in the Church: A Study in Hermeneutics*. Philadelphia: Westminster, 1970.

Stendahl, Krister. "The Apostle Paul and the Introspective Conscience of the West." *Harvard Theological Review* 56 (1963) 199–215; reprinted in Stendahl, *Paul among Jews and Gentiles, and Other Essays*, 78–96. Philadelphia, Fortress, 1976.

Stout, Jeffrey. *Democracy and Tradition: Religion, Ethics, and Public Philosophy*. Princeton: Princeton University Press, 2003.

Swartley, Willard M. *Slavery, Sabbath, War, and Women: Case Issues in Biblical Interpretation*. Scottdale, PA: Herald, 1983.

Thiemann, Ronald F. *Religion in Public Life: A Dilemma for Democracy*. Washingon,DC: Georgetown University Press, l996.

Thompson, Thomas L. *The Bible in History: How Writers Create a Past*. London: Cape, 1999.

————. *Early History of the Israelite People: From the Written and Archaeological Sources*. Studies in the History of the Ancient Near East 4. Leiden: Brill, 2000.

————. *The Mythic Past: Biblical Archaeology and the Myth of Israel*. New York: Basic Books, 1999.

Wildberger, Hans. *Isaiah 1–12: A Commentary*. Translated by Thomas H. Trapp. Continental Commentaries. Minneapolis: Fortress, 1991.

Yoder, John Howard. *The Politics of Jesus*. 2nd ed. Grand Rapids: Eerdmans, 1994.

Scripture Index

Old Testament

Scripture Index

Author Index